JAZZ BIBLE SERIES FAKE BOOK

200 OF THE BEST SONGS FROM
SWING ERA

Compiled and edited by Rob DuBoff

D0898839

Song Index 2
Biographies 231
Artist Index 242

This series would not have been possible without encouragement from my family and friends. Thanks to: Grandma Lydia for helping me brainstorm for prospective titles, Mark Vinci and Mark Davis for sparking my interest in song collection, Jim and Jane Hall for their enthusiasm, Noel Silverman for being my advocate, Doug and Wendy for giving me perspective, and especially my parents, Arlene and Andy, for their tremendous support, confidence and guidance.

Special gratitude to Heather for being my sounding board, problem solver, editor, frequently-more-accurate extra set of ears and most importantly, my best friend. Without your unconditional support this project would not be.

THE JAZZ BIBLE™ and JAZZLINES PUBLICATIONS™ are trademarks used under license from Hero Enterprises, Inc. Compiled and edited by Rob DuBoff for Jazzlines Publications™, a division of Hero Enterprises, Inc.

ISBN 0-7935-5658-9

EXCLUSIVELY DISTRIBUTED BY
HAL•LEONARD® CORPORATION
7777 W. BLUEMOUND RD. P.O. BOX 13819 MILWAUKEE, WI 53213

200 OF THE BEST SONGS FROM
SWING ERA
C O N T E N T S

AIR MAIL SPECIAL	*BENNY GOODMAN*	**11**
ALL OR NOTHING AT ALL	*FRANK SINATRA, JOHN COLTRANE*	**12**
ALL THE THINGS YOU ARE	*TOMMY DORSEY, CHARLIE PARKER*	**14**
ALL THROUGH THE DAY	*FRANK SINATRA*	**15**
APRIL IN PARIS	*GLENN MILLER, COUNT BASIE*	**16**
AREN'T YOU GLAD YOU'RE YOU	*BING CROSBY, MEL TORME*	**17**
BABY, WON'T YOU PLEASE COME HOME	*JIMMIE LUNCEFORD*	**18**
BE CAREFUL, IT'S MY HEART	*FRANK SINATRA*	**19**
BETWEEN THE DEVIL AND THE DEEP BLUE SEA	*BENNY GOODMAN, ELLA FITZGERALD*	**20**
BEWITCHED	*LEO REISMAN, PAUL DESMOND*	**21**
BIJOU	*WOODY HERMAN*	**22**
BLUE AND SENTIMENTAL	*COUNT BASIE*	**23**
BLUE FLAME	*WOODY HERMAN*	**24**
BROADWAY	*COUNT BASIE, DEXTER GORDON*	**25**
BY MYSELF	*FRED ASTAIRE, ART FARMER*	**26**
CANDY	*JOHNNY MERCER, NAT KING COLE*	**27**
CARAVAN	*DUKE ELLINGTON, WES MONTGOMERY*	**28**
CHEEK TO CHEEK	*FRED ASTAIRE, BILLIE HOLIDAY*	**30**
CHELSEA BRIDGE	*DUKE ELLINGTON*	**29**
CHEROKEE (INDIAN LOVE SONG)	*COUNT BASIE, SONNY STITT*	**32**
CLOSE AS PAGES IN A BOOK	*BENNY GOODMAN*	**34**
COME RAIN OR COME SHINE	*MARGARET WHITING, ART TATUM*	**35**
COME SUNDAY	*DUKE ELLINGTON, OSCAR PETERSON*	**36**
DARN THAT DREAM	*MILDRED BAILEY, MILES DAVIS*	**37**
DAY BY DAY	*FRANK SINATRA, LEE MORGAN*	**38**
DEARLY BELOVED	*DINAH SHORE, WES MONTGOMERY*	**39**
DOCTOR JAZZ	*WOODY HERMAN*	**40**
DON'T EXPLAIN	*BILLIE HOLIDAY, CHET BAKER*	**41**
DON'T GET AROUND MUCH ANYMORE	*DUKE ELLINGTON*	**42**
DON'T TAKE YOUR LOVE FROM ME	*GLEN GRAY, JOHN COLTRANE*	**43**
DON'T YOU KNOW I CARE (OR DON'T YOU CARE TO KNOW)	*DUKE ELLINGTON*	**44**
DOWN UNDER	*WOODY HERMAN*	**45**
EASY LIVING	*BILLIE HOLIDAY, CLIFFORD BROWN*	**46**
EASY STREET	*JUNE CHRISTY*	**47**
EASY TO LOVE (A/K/A YOU'D BE SO EASY TO LOVE)	*CHARLIE PARKER*	**48**
EV'RY TIME WE SAY GOODBYE	*STAN KENTON, JOHN COLTRANE*	**49**
EVERYTHING BUT YOU	*DUKE ELLINGTON*	**50**
EVERYTHING HAPPENS TO ME	*TOMMY DORSEY, THELONIOUS MONK*	**51**
EV'RYTHING I LOVE	*PEGGY LEE, BILL EVANS*	**52**
FELLA WITH AN UMBRELLA	*BING CROSBY*	**53**
FINE AND MELLOW	*BILLIE HOLIDAY*	**54**
A FINE ROMANCE	*BILLIE HOLIDAY, ELLA FITZGERALD*	**56**

FLAMINGO	*DUKE ELLINGTON, DIZZY GILLESPIE*	57
THE FOLKS WHO LIVE ON THE HILL	*GUY LOMBARDO*	58
FOOLIN' MYSELF	*BILLIE HOLIDAY*	59
FOR DANCERS ONLY	*JIMMIE LUNCEFORD*	60
FOR YOU, FOR ME, FOR EVERMORE	*JUDY GARLAND + DICK HAYMES*	
	ELLA FITZGERALD	61
FULL MOON AND EMPTY ARMS	*FRANK SINATRA, FREDDIE HUBBARD*	62
GOD BLESS THE CHILD	*BILLIE HOLIDAY, WES MONTGOMERY*	63
GOLDEN EARRINGS	*PEGGY LEE, KENNY DORHAM*	64
GONE WITH THE WIND	*CLIFFORD BROWN*	65
GOOD-BYE	*BENNY GOODMAN, OSCAR PETERSON*	66
A HANDFUL OF STARS	*GLENN MILLER, NAT KING COLE*	67
HEART AND SOUL	*LARRY CLINTON, BETTY CARTER*	68
THE HOUSE I LIVE IN	*FRANK SINATRA, SONNY ROLLINS*	70
HOW ARE THINGS IN GLOCCA MORRA	*BUDDY CLARK, WYNTON MARSALIS*	69
I CAN'T GET STARTED WITH YOU	*BUNNY BERIGAN, CHARLIE PARKER*	72
I CONCENTRATE ON YOU	*TOMMY DORSEY, OSCAR PETERSON*	74
I COULD WRITE A BOOK	*EDDY DUCHIN, MILES DAVIS*	73
I COULDN'T SLEEP A WINK LAST NIGHT	*FRANK SINATRA*	76
I DIDN'T KNOW WHAT TIME IT WAS	*JIMMY DORSEY, CHARLIE PARKER*	77
I DON'T KNOW WHY (I JUST DO)	*SARAH VAUGHAN*	78
I DON'T WANT TO WALK WITHOUT YOU	*ARTIE SHAW*	79
I'VE FOUND A NEW BABY (A/K/A I FOUND A NEW BABY)	*JACK PALMER, SPENCER WILLIAMS*	80
I GOT IT BAD AND THAT AIN'T GOOD	*DUKE ELLINGTON*	81
I GOTTA RIGHT TO SING THE BLUES	*JACK TEAGARDEN, BILLIE HOLIDAY*	82
I HADN'T ANYONE TILL YOU	*RAY NOBLE, BILLIE HOLIDAY*	83
I HEAR A RHAPSODY	*JIMMY DORSEY, BILL EVANS*	84
I JUST FOUND OUT ABOUT LOVE	*DICK HAYMES, SHIRLEY HORN*	85
I LET A SONG GO OUT OF MY HEART	*DUKE ELLINGTON*	86
I LOVE YOU	*JO STAFFORD, JOHN COLTRANE*	87
I REMEMBER YOU	*CANNONBALL ADDERLEY*	88
I SEE YOUR FACE BEFORE ME	*GLEN GRAY, JOHN COLTRANE*	89
I SHOULD CARE	*FRANK SINATRA, BILL EVANS*	90
I WISH I WERE IN LOVE AGAIN	*BING CROSBY, ELLA FITZGERALD*	91
I'LL BE AROUND	*GLENN MILLER, BILLIE HOLIDAY*	92
I'LL BE SEEING YOU	*FRANK SINATRA, BILLIE HOLIDAY*	93
I'LL NEVER SMILE AGAIN	*TOMMY DORSEY, BILL EVANS*	94
I'LL TAKE ROMANCE	*JUNE CHRISTY, CAROL SLOANE*	96
I'LL WALK ALONE	*DINAH SHORE, CHARLIE PARKER*	95
I'M BEGINNING TO SEE THE LIGHT	*HARRY JAMES, DUKE ELLINGTON*	98
I'M GLAD THERE IS YOU (IN THIS WORLD OF ORDINARY PEOPLE)	*JIMMY DORSEY, STAN GETZ*	99
I'M JUST A LUCKY SO AND SO	*DUKE ELLINGTON, WES MONTGOMERY*	100
I'M OLD FASHIONED	*FRED ASTAIRE, JOHN COLTRANE*	101
I'VE GOT MY LOVE TO KEEP ME WARM	*BILLIE HOLIDAY, ELLA FITZGERALD*	102
I'VE GOT YOU UNDER MY SKIN	*RAY NOBLE, BILL EVANS*	104
I'VE HEARD THAT SONG BEFORE	*HARRY JAMES*	103
IF I LOVED YOU	*FRANK SINATRA*	106
IMAGINATION	*TOMMY DORSEY, SARAH VAUGHAN*	107
IN A SENTIMENTAL MOOD	*DUKE ELLINGTON*	108
IN THE BLUE OF EVENING	*TOMMY DORSEY, BENNY GOODMAN*	109
IN THE MOOD	*GLENN MILLER*	110
IN THE STILL OF THE NIGHT	*TOMMY DORSEY, OSCAR PETERSON*	112
IS YOU IS, OR IS YOU AIN'T (MA' BABY)	*LOUIS JORDAN, NAT KING COLE*	114
IT COULD HAPPEN TO YOU	*JO STAFFORD, MILES DAVIS*	116

4

IT MIGHT AS WELL BE SPRING	*DICK HAYMES, KENNY DORHAM*	**117**
IT NEVER ENTERED MY MIND	*DAVID ALLYN, FRANK SINATRA*	**118**
IT'S A BLUE WORLD	*TONY MARTIN, COLEMAN HAWKINS*	**119**
IT'S BEEN A LONG, LONG TIME	*HARRY JAMES, LOUIS ARMSTRONG*	**120**
IT'S ONLY A PAPER MOON	*ELLA FITZGERALD, MILES DAVIS*	**121**
JERSEY BOUNCE	*BENNY GOODMAN, ELLA FITZGERALD*	**122**
JITTERBUG WALTZ	*FATS WALLER, ART TATUM*	**124**
JOHNNY COME LATELY	*DUKE ELLINGTON*	**123**
JUNE IN JANUARY	*BING.CROSBY, ART FARMER*	**126**
THE LADY IS A TRAMP	*TOMMY DORSEY, ELLA FITZGERALD*	**127**
THE LADY'S IN LOVE WITH YOU	*BENNY GOODMAN, JIMMY ROWLES*	**128**
THE LAST TIME I SAW PARIS	*HILDEGARDE, MICHEL LEGRAND*	**129**
LET'S GET AWAY FROM IT ALL	*TOMMY DORSEY*	**130**
LET'S GET LOST	*TEDDY POWELL, CHET BAKER*	**131**
LET'S HAVE ANOTHER CUP O' COFFEE	*ETHEL MERMAN*	**132**
LIKE SOMEONE IN LOVE	*BING CROSBY, JOHN COLTRANE*	**133**
LONG AGO (AND FAR AWAY)	*JO STAFFORD, STITT/AMMONS*	**134**
A LOVELY WAY TO SPEND AN EVENING	*GLENN MILLER, TORME/SHEARING*	**135**
LOVER MAN (OH, WHERE CAN YOU BE?)	*BILLIE HOLIDAY, CHARLIE PARKER*	**136**
MARIE	*TOMMY DORSEY*	**137**
(I'M AFRAID) THE MASQUERADE IS OVER	*LARRY CLINTON, GEORGE BENSON*	**138**
MOONLIGHT BECOMES YOU	*GLENN MILLER, GEORGE SHEARING*	**140**
MOONLIGHT IN VERMONT	*ELLA FITZGERALD*	**141**
MY FUNNY VALENTINE	*LEE WILEY, MILES DAVIS*	**142**
MY HEART BELONGS TO DADDY	*MARY MARTIN, CHARLIE PARKER*	**143**
MY LAST AFFAIR	*MILDRED BAILEY, ELLA FITZGERALD*	**144**
MY SHINING HOUR	*FRED ASTAIRE, JOHN COLTRANE*	**145**
MY SHIP	*GERTRUDE LAWRENCE, MILES DAVIS*	**146**
MY SILENT LOVE	*HARRY JAMES, ZOOT SIMS*	**147**
THE NEARNESS OF YOU	*CONNEE BOSWELL, ABBEY LINCOLN*	**148**
A NIGHTINGALE SANG IN BERKELEY SQUARE	*GLENN MILLER, DEXTER GORDON*	**149**
THE NIGHT WE CALLED IT A DAY	*TOMMY DORSEY, JOHN COLTRANE*	**150**
NO MORE	*BILLIE HOLIDAY, TOMMY FLANAGAN*	**151**
NOBODY'S HEART	*MEL TORME*	**152**
NUAGES	*DJANGO REINHARDT*	**153**
ON A SLOW BOAT TO CHINA	*KAY KYSER, CHARLIE PARKER*	**158**
ONE FOR MY BABY (AND ONE MORE FOR THE ROAD)	*JOHNNY MERCER, FRANK SINATRA*	**154**
OUT OF THIS WORLD	*BING CROSBY, JOHN COLTRANE*	**156**
PENNIES FROM HEAVEN	*BING CROSBY, ZOOT SIMS*	**159**
PEOPLE WILL SAY WE'RE IN LOVE	*FRANK SINATRA*	**160**
POINCIANA (SONG OF THE TREE)	*GLENN MILLER, AHMAD JAMAL*	**161**
POLKA DOTS AND MOONBEAMS	*TOMMY DORSEY, PAUL DESMOND*	**162**
PRELUDE TO A KISS	*DUKE ELLINGTON, BILLIE HOLIDAY*	**163**
RAIN CHECK	*DUKE ELLINGTON, ART FARMER*	**164**
RIDIN' HIGH	*BENNY GOODMAN, ELLA FITZGERALD*	**166**
RIGHT AS THE RAIN	*LENA HORNE, MAUREEN McGOVERN*	**165**
RUSSIAN LULLABY	*BING CROSBY, JOHN COLTRANE*	**168**
SATURDAY NIGHT IS THE LONELIEST NIGHT OF THE WEEK	*FRANK SINATRA, OSCAR PETERSON*	**169**
SAY IT (OVER AND OVER AGAIN)	*JOHN COLTRANE*	**170**
SENTIMENTAL JOURNEY	*LES BROWN, S. GETZ/ J. SMITH*	**171**
A SINNER KISSED AN ANGEL	*HARRY JAMES, GEORGE SHEARING*	**172**
SKYLARK	*BILLY ECKSTINE, STAN GETZ*	**173**

SLEEPY LAGOON	*HARRY JAMES*	**174**
SOMEDAY MY PRINCE WILL COME	*OSCAR PETERSON, BILL EVANS*	**175**
SOMETHING I DREAMED LAST NIGHT	*ELLA LOGAN, MILES DAVIS*	**176**
SOMETHING TO LIVE FOR	*DUKE ELLINGTON, CAROL SLOANE*	**177**
SPEAK LOW	*GLENN MILLER, McCOY TYNER*	**178**
THE STAR-CROSSED LOVERS	*DUKE ELLINGTON*	**180**
STOMPIN' AT THE SAVOY	*BENNY GOODMAN, ELLA FITZGERALD*	**181**
STORMY WEATHER (KEEPS RAININ' ALL THE TIME)	*ETHEL WATERS, FRANK SINATRA*	**182**
A STRING OF PEARLS	*GLENN MILLER*	**183**
SUNRISE SERENADE	*GLENN MILLER*	**184**
THE SURREY WITH THE FRINGE ON TOP	*MILES DAVIS*	**185**
SWEET AND LOVELY	*WOODY HERMAN, McCOY TYNER*	**186**
SWINGING ON A STAR	*BING CROSBY, OSCAR PETERSON*	**187**
TAKE THE 'A' TRAIN	*DUKE ELLINGTON, DIZZY GILLESPIE*	**188**
TANGERINE	*JIMMY DORSEY, GENE AMMONS*	**189**
THANKS FOR THE MEMORY	*MILDRED BAILEY, STAN GETZ*	**190**
THAT OLD BLACK MAGIC	*BING CROSBY, ELLA FITZGERALD*	**192**
THAT OLD FEELING	*SHEP FIELDS, TEDDY WILSON*	**191**
THAT OLE DEVIL CALLED LOVE	*BILLIE HOLIDAY, CHET BAKER*	**194**
THEM THERE EYES	*BILLIE HOLIDAY, ELLA FITZGERALD*	**195**
THERE IS NO GREATER LOVE	*STAN KENTON, MILES DAVIS*	**196**
THERE WILL NEVER BE ANOTHER YOU	*WOODY HERMAN, SONNY ROLLINS*	**197**
THERE'S A SMALL HOTEL	*BENNY GOODMAN, JOHNNY SMITH*	**198**
THESE FOOLISH THINGS (REMIND ME OF YOU)	*BILLIE HOLIDAY, ELLA FITZGERALD*	**199**
THINGS AIN'T WHAT THEY USED TO BE	*DUKE ELLINGTON*	**200**
THINKING OF YOU	*FRED ASTAIRE, SARAH VAUGHAN*	**201**
THIS CAN'T BE LOVE	*CANNONBALL ADDERLEY*	**202**
THIS LOVE OF MINE	*TOMMY DORSEY, SONNY ROLLINS*	**203**
THIS YEAR'S KISSES	*BILLIE HOLIDAY, TEDDY WILSON*	**204**
TUXEDO JUNCTION	*ERSKINE HAWKINS, GEORGE BENSON*	**205**
UNDECIDED	*BENNY GOODMAN*	**206**
UNTIL THE REAL THING COMES ALONG	*ANDY KIRK, BILLIE HOLIDAY*	**207**
UP WITH THE LARK	*BILL EVANS*	**208**
THE VERY THOUGHT OF YOU	*BING CROSBY, TOMMY FLANAGAN*	**210**
VIOLETS FOR YOUR FURS	*GENE KRUPA, BILLIE HOLIDAY*	**211**
WAIT TILL YOU SEE HER	*DAVID ALLYN, PHIL WOODS*	**212**
WHAT A DIFF'RENCE A DAY MADE	*DINAH WASHINGTON*	**213**
WHEN YOU WISH UPON A STAR	*CLIFF EDWARDS, BILL EVANS*	**214**
WHERE OR WHEN	*CLIFFORD BROWN*	**215**
WHO?	*TOMMY DORSEY*	**216**
WHO WOULDN'T LOVE YOU	*KAY KYSER*	**217**
WHY CAN'T I?	*SARAH VAUGHAN*	**218**
WHY DON'T YOU DO RIGHT (GET ME SOME MONEY, TOO!)	*PEGGY LEE, ELLA FITZGERALD*	**219**
WILD ROOT	*WOODY HERMAN*	**222**
WILL YOU STILL BE MINE	*TOMMY DORSEY, SONNY ROLLINS*	**220**
WILLOW WEEP FOR ME	*JUNE CHRISTY, DEXTER GORDON*	**223**
YES INDEED	*TOMMY DORSEY, RON CARTER*	**224**
YOU DON'T KNOW WHAT LOVE IS	*BILLIE HOLIDAY, JOHN COLTRANE*	**225**
YOU TURNED THE TABLES ON ME	*BENNY GOODMAN, KENNY BURRELL*	**226**
YOU'D BE SO NICE TO COME HOME TO	*DINAH SHORE, ELLA FITZGERALD*	**227**
YOU'RE BLASÉ	*SARAH VAUGHAN, STAN GETZ*	**228**
YOU'RE EASY TO DANCE WITH	*PEGGY LEE*	**229**
YOU'RE NEARER	*CAROL SLOANE*	**230**

FOREWORD

There are many publications called "fake books" in the music marketplace today. A fake book provides a collection of many standard and popular songs that are, in many cases, difficult to obtain. Unfortunately, fake books often utilize simplified or incorrect harmonies. When we are dealing with the music of many publishers over a period of a century, we often run into various differences in chord naming, notation and general editorial policy. Simply stated, many songs have come down to us with incorrect harmony and antiquated rhythmic notation. Often composers were consulted when their songs were prepared for sheet music editions, and a few even wrote their own piano/vocal arrangements for publication. But many established composers did not; so, many songs have been continuously available in arrangements that are not properly representative.

The idea of the 'standard classic song' is a relatively new one in American music. It was Frank Sinatra who popularized the performance of songs that were not current hit parade material, and even recorded them in 78 (and later 33 1/3) albums. In turn, jazz musicians and singers learned and collected the classic songs of Kern, Gershwin, Rodgers and Porter. Much of this repertoire was learned from recordings. The songs were often harmonically recomposed to make them more interesting for improvisation. In recent years, students seeking to learn these standards have similarly transcribed their favorite recordings. We felt that there should be a series of volumes containing the greatest popular songs with accurate melodies, chord progressions and lyrics. The Jazz Bible™ Series is the result.

The process for choosing titles to include was not complicated. A list of the 1000 most widely performed jazz standards was drafted, then evenly divided into five volumes, each representing a period of jazz. These volumes are:

RAGTIME AND EARLY JAZZ (1900-35)
THE SWING ERA (1936-47)
THE BEBOP ERA (1947-55)
JAZZ IN THE '50s (1950-59)
JAZZ IN THE '60s AND BEYOND (1960 - Present)

Generally, a song was placed in the era when it became popular, not necessarily when it was written. Unfortunately, several songs could not be included due to copyright restrictions.

Once the master title list was completed, the job of locating sources for each of the songs began. This proved to be a more complicated task than was first imagined. Songs were found in numerous libraries, such as The Library of Congress, The Smithsonian Archives, The Library of the Performing Arts at Lincoln Center, and many private collections throughout the United States. A number of these songs were quite rare, and some had to be assembled from scores or sketches. We then began listening to key recordings of these songs, with particular attention to classic jazz performances. (It was quite interesting to witness the metamorphosis of a song over many years of performances.) Through this research, we compiled the most commonly used chords for each song, many of which differed dramatically from the original sources. We refer to these substitute chords as the *adopted chord changes*. One of the difficulties in transcribing chord changes is distinguishing between harmonies that are commonly played and those that have been specifically arranged for a recording. To this end we have compared the adopted chord changes to the originals to ensure harmonic accuracy.

We have insured that this book be user-friendly by developing the following layout:

Generally, only one song is printed per page
A four-bar-to-a-line format has been used whenever possible
The form of each song can be seen at a glance with section
     marks that can also double as rehearsal letters

The volumes also include a chord glossary and biographies of many of the composers and lyricists.

CHORDS

There were many cases where we felt it was appropriate to include both the original and the adopted set of chords. The adopted chords appear in italics above the original chords. Where only italicized chords appear in any measure or an italicized chord with no other chord underneath, the original music had the previous chord continuing. In some cases the adopted chords clash with the melody; these instances are noted. We have also included turnaround chords at the end of every song; these are always italicized. A chord with the suffix *alt* implies that any altered chord can be substituted. (Please see the chord glossary for possible altered chords.)

FORM

The form of every song is clearly outlined with the use of section marks, each musically distinct section labeled a different letter. Where there is a section that is a variation of a preceding one, we have labeled the varying section with a superscript number. For example, A A^1 B A^2 would indicate that the form is A A B A with the second A varying slightly from the first A and the last A another variation. In cases where the verse to a song has been included, it is labeled V; an introduction is labeled I.

Naturally, each tune is open to difference in interpretation, and one should never rely solely on one source (be it printed or recorded) for learning songs. There is absolutely no substitute for developing one's ear through harmonic and melodic ear training, playing with others and listening to recordings.

We would be happy to hear your comments and criticisms, which will affect future editions in this series. An address is provided below.

Much research and thought went into the creation of this series, insuring that these fakebooks set new standards in printed music. They were undertaken with one thought in mind: you, the musician, should have the best possible printed sources for the finest songs of this century. I feel privileged to have been given the opportunity to work on this project. Thanks to Jim and Jane Hall, Noel Silverman, John Cerullo, Keith Mardak, and especially, Jeff Sultanof.

Robert DuBoff
C/O Hero Enterprises, Inc.
P.O. Box 1236
Saratoga Springs, NY 12866-0887

Please note that this is a **legal** fake book; **all fake books that do not display song copyright and ownership information somewhere on each title page are illegal.** Such publications violate U.S. intellectual property law by not reimbursing copyright owners for the use of their songs. Please help stop such infringements; do not buy these publications.

Rhythm Changes

(Based on the chord changes to "I Got Rhythm")

Blues Changes

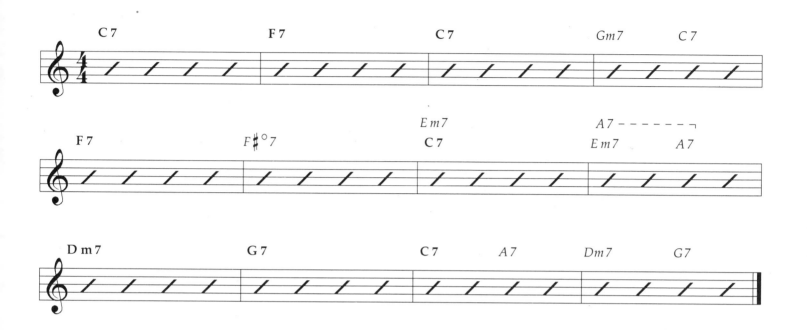

Minor Blues Changes

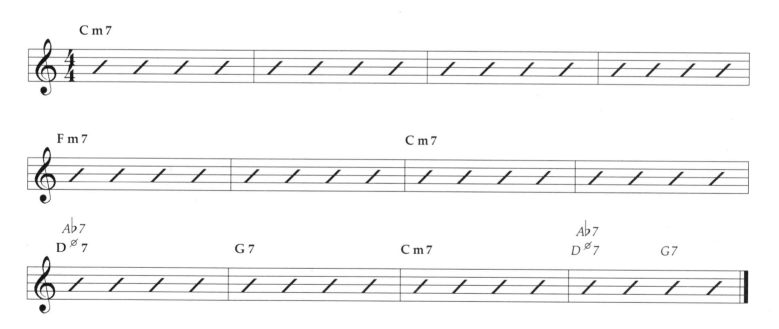

Chord Glossary

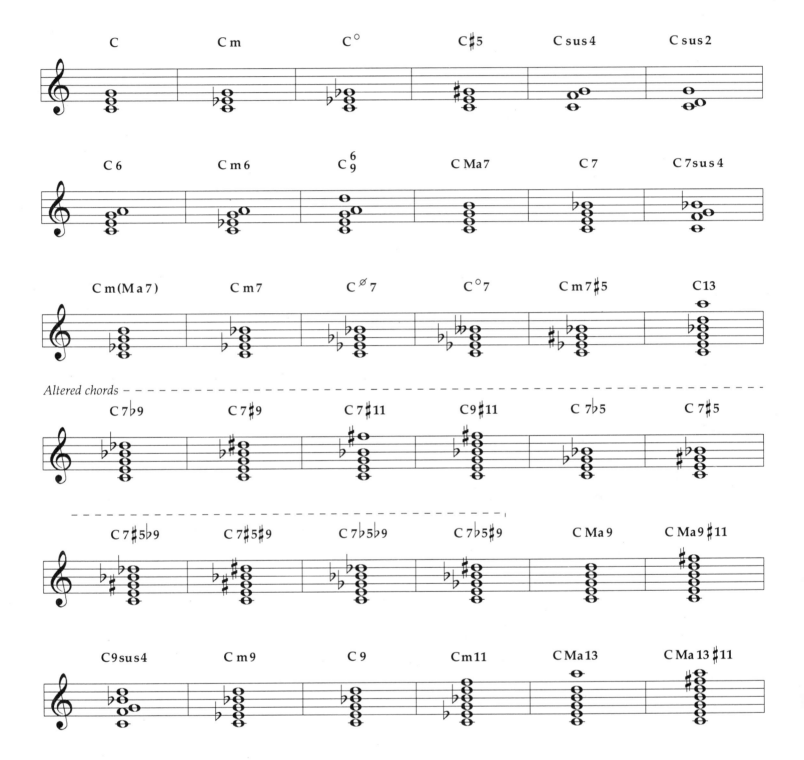

Air Mail Special

Bright

By Benny Goodman, Jimmy Mundy
and Charlie Christian

Note: The italicized chords are used for solos only.

All or Nothing at All

Words by Jack Lawrence
Music by Arthur Altman

All the Things You Are

Lyrics by Oscar Hammerstein II
Music by Jerome Kern

Medium

All through the Day

Medium

Lyrics by Oscar Hammerstein II
Music by Jerome Kern

April in Paris

Words by E.Y. Harburg
Music by Vernon Duke

Medium

Aren't You Glad You're You

Medium

Words by Johnny Burke
Music by Jimmy Van Heusen

Baby, Won't You Please Come Home

Words and Music by Charles Warfield
and Clarence Williams

Medium

Be Careful, It's My Heart

Medium

Words and Music by
Irving Berlin

Between the Devil and the Deep Blue Sea

Medium

Lyric by Ted Koehler
Music by Harold Arlen

Bewitched

Ballad or Medium

Words by Lorenz Hart
Music by Richard Rodgers

Note: In each lyric bracket,
the original lyrics are italicized.

Bijou

Medium

Music by
Ralph Burns

Blue and Sentimental

Words and Music by Mack David,
Jerry Livingston and Count Basie

Ballad

Blue Flame

Lyric by Leo Corday
Music by James Noble and Joe Bishop

Ballad

Blue flame, lone-ly mem-'ries, light-ing my heart.

Blue flame, on-ly mem-'ries, why did we part? Ev-er

burn-ing, ev-er yearn-ing blue flame.

Blue flame, burn-ing sor-row, deep in my heart.

Blue flame will to-mor-row bring a new start. Ev-er

glow-ing, ev-er grow-ing blue flame.

Note: For solos use standard blues changes in B flat (see "Blues Changes").

Broadway

Bright

By Bill Byrd,
Teddy McRae and Henri Woode

By Myself

Words by Howard Dietz
Music by Arthur Schwartz

Medium

Candy

Medium

Words and Music by Mack David,
Joan Whitney and Alex Kramer

Caravan

Medium

Words and Music by Duke Ellington,
Irving Mills and Juan Tizol

Note: The grace note melody is
used for instrumental versions.

Chelsea Bridge

Ballad

Music by
Billy Strayhorn

Cheek to Cheek

Words and Music by
Irving Berlin

Medium

C C m 7   A♭7

Dance with me._____ I want my arms a-bout you._____ The

G 7   *Em 7*   C Ma7/E   A 7   D m 7   G 7

charm a-bout you_____ will car - ry me thru_____ to

A C Ma7   A m 7   D m 7   G 7   C Ma7   A m 7   D m 7   G 7

heav - en._____ I'm in heav - en,_____ and my

C Ma7   D m 7   E♭°7   C Ma7/E   B♭7♯11   A 7

heart beats so that I can hard - ly speak,_____ and I

D m 7   G 7   B♭7♯11   A 7

seem to find the hap - pi - ness I seek_____ when we're

D m 7   G 7   C Ma7   *Am 7*   *Dm 7*   *G 7*

out to-geth - er danc - ing cheek__ to cheek.__

Cherokee
(Indian Love Song)

Words and Music by
Ray Noble

Bright

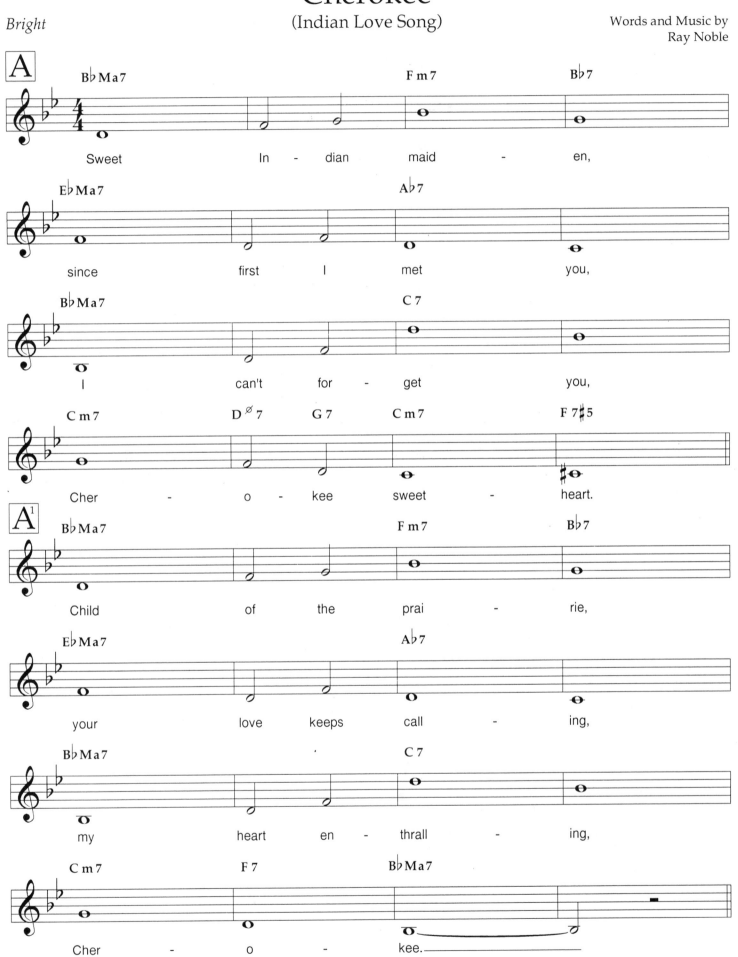

Close as Pages in a Book

Medium

Words by Dorothy Fields
Music by Sigmund Romberg

Come Rain or Come Shine

Medium

Words by Johnny Mercer
Music by Harold Arlen

Come Sunday

Ballad

By Duke Ellington

Darn That Dream

Ballad

Lyric by Eddie DeLange
Music by Jimmy Van Heusen

Day by Day

Medium

Words and Music by Sammy Cahn,
Axel Stordahl and Paul Weston

Dearly Beloved

Medium or Bright

Words by Johnny Mercer
Music by Jerome Kern

Doctor Jazz

Lyric by Walter Melrose
Music by Joseph 'King' Oliver

Medium

Don't Explain

Ballad or Medium

Words and Music by Billie Holiday
and Arthur Herzog

MCA music publishing

Don't Get around Much Anymore

Words and Music by Bob Russell
and Duke Ellington

Missed the Sat-ur-day dance,_____ heard they crowd-ed the floor_____

could-n't bear it with-out_____ you,_____
they'd have asked me a-bout_____ you,_____

got as far as the door,_____

don't get a-round much an-y-

more. Thought I'd vis-it the club,___ more_____

Dar-ling I guess_____ my mind's more at ease,_____ but

nev-er-the-less,_____ why stir up mem-o-ries?_____ Been in-vit-ed on dates,_____

might have gone but what for?_____ Aw-f'lly dif-f'rent with-out_____

_____ you,_____ don't get a-round much an-y-more.

Don't Take Your Love from Me

Ballad

Words and Music by
Henry Nemo

Don't You Know I Care
(Or Don't You Care to Know)

Words by Mack David
Music by Duke Ellington

Ballad

Down Under

Bright

By Dizzy Gillespie

Easy Living

Ballad

Words and Music by Leo Robin
and Ralph Rainger

Easy Street

Ballad or Medium

By Alan Rankin Jones

Easy to Love

(a/k/a You'd Be So Easy to Love)

Words and Music by
Cole Porter

Medium

Ev'ry Time We Say Goodbye

Ballad

Words and Music by
Cole Porter

Everything but You

Medium

By Duke Ellington, Harry James
and Don George

A

You left me a horse— from Tex- as,— a house with in- stal - ments due,— a

let- ter with lots— of X - S,— ev - 'ry- thing but you.— You

A

left me some beans— from Bos- ton,— a bi- cy- cle built— for two,— a

mem- o - ry to— get lost in,— ev - 'ry- thing but you.

B

Each day— was so gay— and so dar- ing, I loved— ev- 'ry breath— tak- ing min- ute,

for how— could I know— I was shar - ing a kiss with- out a fut - ure in it. You

A

left me a dream— to room with,— a cof- fee pot from— Pe - ru,— a

knife and a fork— to spoon with,— ev - 'ry- thing but you.—

Everything Happens to Me

Ballad

Words by Tom Adair
Music by Matt Dennis

Ev'rything I Love

Words and Music by
Cole Porter

Fella with an Umbrella

Medium

Words and Music by
Irving Berlin

Fine and Mellow

Words and Music by
Billie Holiday

Ballad

A Fine Romance

Medium

Words by Dorothy Fields
Music by Jerome Kern

Flamingo

Lyric by Ed Anderson
Music by Ted Grouya

The Folks Who Live on the Hill

Ballad

Lyrics by Oscar Hammerstein II
Music by Jerome Kern

Foolin' Myself

Medium

By Jack Lawrence
and Peter Tinturin

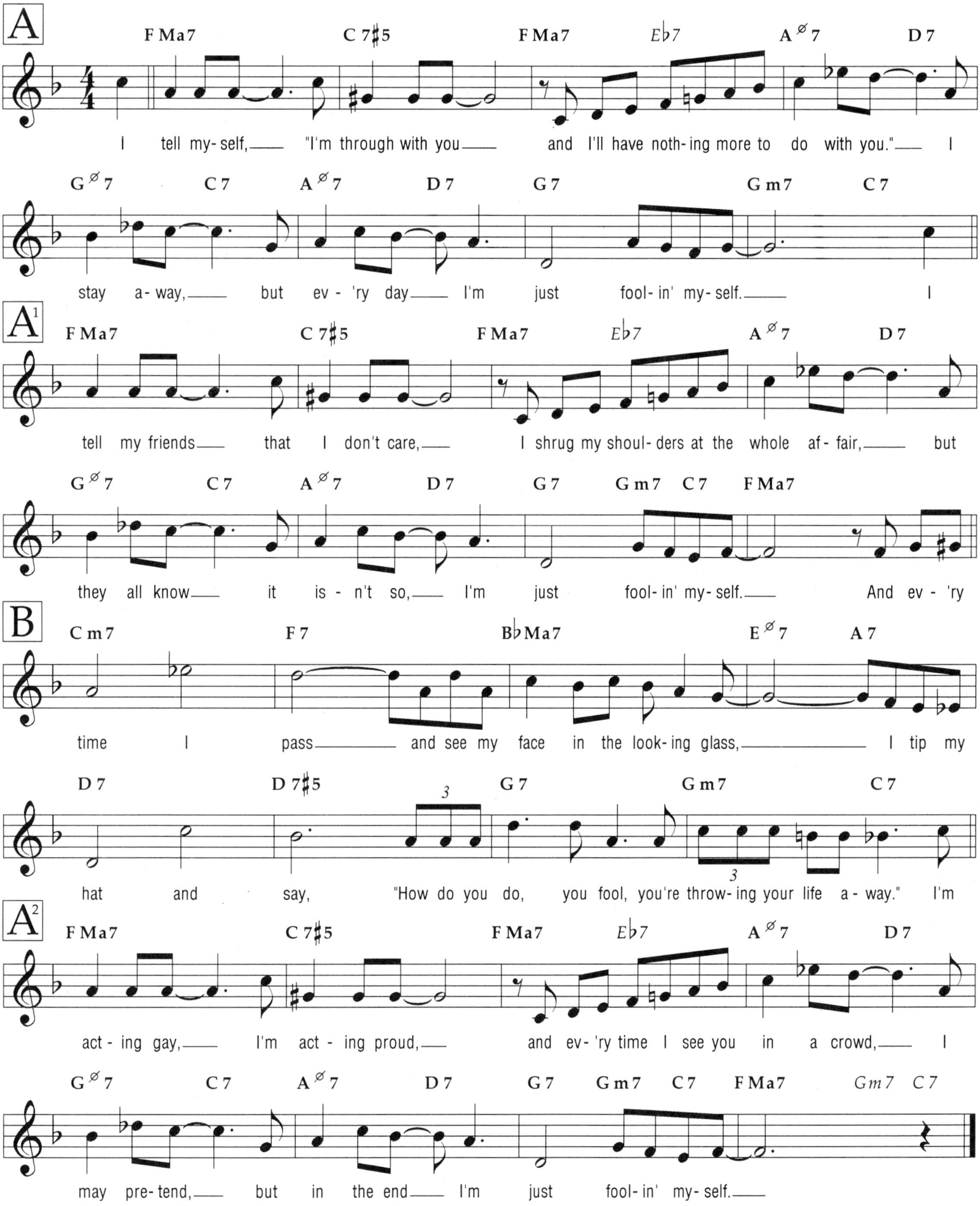

A
F Ma7 C 7♯5 F Ma7 E♭7 A ø7 D 7
I tell my-self, "I'm through with you and I'll have noth-ing more to do with you." I
G ø7 C 7 A ø7 D 7 G 7 G m7 C 7
stay a-way, but ev-'ry day I'm just fool-in' my-self. I
A1
F Ma7 C 7♯5 F Ma7 E♭7 A ø7 D 7
tell my friends that I don't care, I shrug my shoul-ders at the whole af-fair, but
G ø7 C 7 A ø7 D 7 G 7 G m7 C 7 F Ma7
they all know it is-n't so, I'm just fool-in' my-self. And ev-'ry
B
C m7 F 7 B♭Ma7 E ø7 A 7
time I pass and see my face in the look-ing glass, I tip my
D 7 D 7♯5 G 7 G m7 C 7
3
hat and say, "How do you do, you fool, you're throw-ing your life a-way." I'm
3
A2
F Ma7 C 7♯5 F Ma7 E♭7 A ø7 D 7
act-ing gay, I'm act-ing proud, and ev-'ry time I see you in a crowd, I
G ø7 C 7 A ø7 D 7 G 7 G m7 C 7 F Ma7 Gm7 C7
may pre-tend, but in the end I'm just fool-in' my-self.

For Dancers Only

Medium

Words by Don Raye and Vic Schoen
Music by Sy Oliver

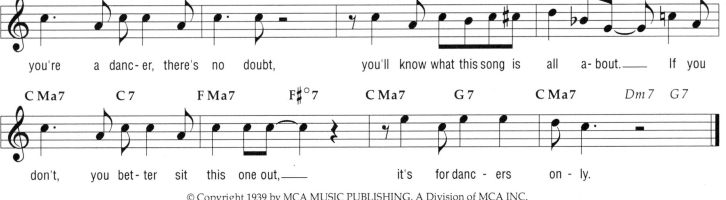

For You, for Me, for Evermore

Medium

Music and Lyrics by George Gershwin
and Ira Gershwin

Full Moon and Empty Arms

Ballad or Medium

Words and Music by Buddy Kaye
and Ted Mossman

God Bless' the Child

Ballad

Words and Music by Arthur Herzog Jr.
and Billie Holiday

Golden Earrings

Medium

Words by Jay Livingston and Ray Evans
Music by Victor Young

Gone with the Wind

Medium

Words and Music by Herb Magidson
and Allie Wrubel

Good-Bye

Ballad

Words and Music by
Gordon Jenkins

A Handful of Stars

Ballad

By Jack Lawrence
and Ted Shapiro

Heart and Soul

Words by Frank Loesser
Music by Hoagy Carmichael

How Are Things in Glocca Morra

Ballad

Words by E.Y. Harburg
Music by Burton Lane

The House I Live In

Medium

Words by Lewis Allen
Music by Earl Robinson

I Can't Get Started with You

Ballad

Words by Ira Gershwin
Music by Vernon Duke

I Could Write a Book

Medium

Words by Lorenz Hart
Music by Richard Rodgers

I Concentrate on You

Medium

Words and Music by
Cole Porter

I Couldn't Sleep a Wink Last Night

Ballad

Words by Harold Adamson
Music by Jimmy McHugh

I Didn't Know What Time It Was

Medium

Words by Lorenz Hart
Music by Richard Rodgers

I Don't Know Why
(I Just Do)

Words by Roy Turk
Music by Fred Ahlert

Ballad

I Don't Want to Walk Without You

Medium

Words by Frank Loesser
Music by Jule Styne

I've Found a New Baby

(a/k/a I Found a New Baby)

Medium

Words and Music by Jack Palmer
and Spencer Williams

I Got It Bad and That Ain't Good

Words by Paul Francis Webster
Music by Duke Ellington

Ballad

I Gotta Right to Sing the Blues

Medium

Words by Ted Koehler
Music by Harold Arlen

I Hadn't Anyone till You

Medium

Words and Music by
Ray Noble

I Hear a Rhapsody

Medium

By George Frajos,
Jack Baker and Dick Gasparre

I Just Found out About Love

Medium

Words and Music by Jimmy McHugh
and Harold Adamson

I Let a Song Go out of My Heart

Medium

Words and Music by Duke Ellington,
Henry Nemo, John Redmond
and Irving Mills

I Love You

Bright

Words and Music by
Cole Porter

I Remember You

Words by Johnny Mercer
Music by Victor Schertzinger

Medium

I See Your Face before Me

Ballad

Words by Howard Dietz
Music by Arthur Schwartz

I Should Care

Ballad

Words and Music by Sammy Cahn,
Axel Stordahl and Paul Weston

I Wish I Were in Love Again

Words by Lorenz Hart
Music by Richard Rodgers

Medium

I'll Be Around

Words and Music by
Alec Wilder

I'll Be Seeing You

Lyric by Irving Kahal
Music by Sammy Fain

Medium

I'll Never Smile Again

Medium

Words and Music by
Ruth Lowe

MCA music publishing

I'll Walk Alone

Ballad

Lyric by Sammy Cahn
Music by Jule Styne

I'll Take Romance

Medium

Lyrics by Oscar Hammerstein II
Music by Ben Oakland

Note: This song is also played in 4/4.

I'm Beginning to See the Light

Medium

Words and Music by Don George, Johnny Hodges,
Duke Ellington and Harry James

I'm Glad There Is You
(In This World of Ordinary People)

Words and Music by Paul Madeira
and Jimmy Dorsey

I'm Just a Lucky So and So

Medium

Words by Mack David
Music by Duke Ellington

I'm Old Fashioned

Ballad or Medium

Words by Johnny Mercer
Music by Jerome Kern

I've Got My Love to Keep Me Warm

Words and Music by
Irving Berlin

I've Heard That Song Before

Medium

Lyric by Sammy Cahn
Music by Jule Styne

I've Got You Under My Skin

Words and Music by
Cole Porter

If I Loved You

Medium

Lyrics by Oscar Hammerstein II
Music by Richard Rodgers

Imagination

Words by Johnny Burke
Music by Jimmy Van Heusen

Ballad

In a Sentimental Mood

Ballad

Words and Music by Duke Ellington,
Irving Mills and Manny Kurtz

In the Blue of Evening

Ballad

Words by Tom Adair
Music by D'Artega

In the Mood

Medium

By Joe Garland

theres a mess of moon-light, won't-cha share it with me?"___ "Well," she ans-wered, "Mis-ter, don't-cha

know that it's rude___ to keep___ my two lips wait-in' when they're in the mood?"___

B

In the mood,___ that's what she told me, in the mood.___ And when she told me

in the mood,___ my heart was skip-pin', it did-n't take me long to say "I'm in the mood___ now!"

B

In the mood___ (Oh joy!)___ for all her kiss-in'. In the mood___ (Oh joy!)___ her cra-zy lov-in',

in the mood.___ (Oh boy!)___ What I was miss-in' it did-n't take me long to say I'm in the mood___ now.

Interlude (No Chord)

In the Still of the Night

Medium

Words and Music by
Cole Porter

Is You Is, or Is You Ain't
(Ma' Baby)

Medium

Words and Music by Billy Austin
and Louis Jordan

It Could Happen to You

Medium

Words by Johnny Burke
Music by Jimmy Van Heusen

It Might as Well Be Spring

Lyrics by Oscar Hammerstein II
Music by Richard Rodgers

It Never Entered My Mind

Words by Lorenz Hart
Music by Richard Rodgers

Note: There are many variations of the chord changes to
this song. These chords are most often played.

It's a Blue World

Medium

Words and Music by Robert Wright
and George Forrest

It's Been a Long, Long Time

Lyric by Sammy Cahn
Music by Jule Styne

Ballad

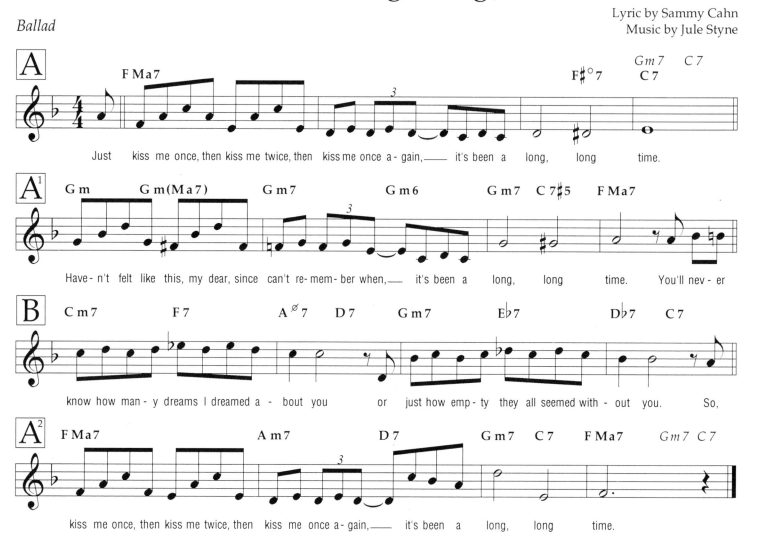

It's Only a Paper Moon

Medium

Lyric by Billy Rose and E.Y. Harburg
Music by Harold Arlen

Jersey Bounce

Words by Robert Wright
Music by Bobby Plater, Tiny Bradshaw,
Edward Johnson and Robert Wright

Medium

Johnny Come Lately

Medium

Music by
Billy Strayhorn

Jitterbug Waltz

Medium

Music by Thomas "Fats" Waller
Lyrics by Richard Maltby

June in January

Medium

Words and Music by Leo Robin
and Ralph Rainger

The Lady Is a Tramp

Medium

Words by Lorenz Hart
Music by Richard Rodgers

The Lady's in Love with You

Medium

Words by Frank Loesser
Music by Burton Lane

The Last Time I Saw Paris

Medium

Lyrics by Oscar Hammerstein II
Music by Jerome Kern

Let's Get Away from It All

Medium

Words and Music by Tom Adair
and Matt Dennis

Let's Get Lost

Medium

Words by Frank Loesser
Music by Jimmy McHugh

Let's Have Another Cup o' Coffee

Medium

Words and Music by
Irving Berlin

Like Someone in Love

Medium

Words by Johnny Burke
Music by Jimmy Van Heusen

Long Ago
(And Far Away)

Ballad or Medium

Words by Ira Gershwin
Music by Jerome Kern

A Lovely Way to Spend an Evening

Ballad

Words by Harold Adamson
Music by Jimmy McHugh

Lover Man
(Oh, Where Can You Be?)

By Jimmy Davis,
Roger "Ram" Ramirez and Jimmy Sherman

Ballad

Marie

Medium

Words and Music by
Irving Berlin

(I'm Afraid)
The Masquerade Is Over

Ballad

Words by Herb Magidson
Music by Allie Wrubel

Moonlight Becomes You

Ballad

Words by Johnny Burke
Music by Jimmy Van Heusen

Copyright © 1942 (Renewed 1970) by Famous Music Corporation
International Copyright Secured   All Rights Reserved

Moonlight in Vermont

Ballad or Medium

Words and Music by John Blackburn
and Karl Suessdorf

My Funny Valentine

Words by Lorenz Hart
Music by Richard Rodgers

Ballad

My Heart Belongs to Daddy

Medium

Words and Music by
Cole Porter

My Last Affair

Medium

By Haven S. Johnson

My Shining Hour

Bright

Lyric by Johnny Mercer
Music by Harold Arlen

My Ship

Words by Ira Gershwin
Music by Kurt Weill

Ballad or Medium

My Silent Love

Medium

Words by Edward Heyman
Music by Dana Suesse

The Nearness of You

Words by Ned Washington
Music by Hoagy Carmichael

A Nightingale Sang in Berkeley Square

Lyric by Eric Maschwitz
Music by Manning Sherwin

The Night We Called It a Day

By Tom Adair
and Matt Dennis

Medium

No More

Ballad

By Bob Russell
and Toots Camarata

Nobody's Heart

Ballad

Words by Lorenz Hart
Music by Richard Rodgers

Nuages

Ballad

By Django Reinhardt
and Jacques Larue

One for My Baby
(And One More for the Road)

Ballad

Lyric by Johnny Mercer
Music by Harold Arlen

Out of This World

Medium

Lyric by Johnny Mercer
Music by Harold Arlen

On a Slow Boat to China

By Frank Loesser

Pennies from Heaven

Words by John Burke
Music by Arthur Johnston

Medium

People Will Say We're in Love

Bright

Lyrics by Oscar Hammerstein II
Music by Richard Rodgers

Poinciana
(Song of the Tree)

Ballad or Medium

Words by Buddy Bernier
Music by Nat Simon

Polka Dots and Moonbeams

Ballad or Medium

Words by Johnny Burke
Music by Jimmy Van Heusen

Prelude to a Kiss

Ballad

Words by Irving Gordon and Irving Mills
Music by Duke Ellington

Rain Check

Medium

Music by
Billy Strayhorn

Right as the Rain

Ballad

Words by E.Y. Harburg
Music by Harold Arlen

Ridin' High

Bright

Words and Music by
Cole Porter

Russian Lullaby

Bright

Words and Music by
Irving Berlin

Note: This song was originally written in 3/4 time.

Saturday Night Is the Loneliest Night of the Week

Medium

Words by Sammy Cahn
Music by Jule Styne

Say It
(Over and over Again)

Words by Frank Loesser and Jimmy McHugh
Music by Jimmy McHugh

Ballad

Sentimental Journey

Medium

By Bud Green,
Les Brown and Ben Homer

A Sinner Kissed an Angel

Ballad

Words by Mack David
Music by Ray Joseph

Skylark

Ballad

Words by Johnny Mercer
Music by Hoagy Carmichael

Sleepy Lagoon

Words by Jack Lawrence
Music by Eric Coates

Note: This song was originally written in 3/4 time.

Someday My Prince Will Come

Medium

Words by Larry Morey
Music by Frank Churchill

Something I Dreamed Last Night

Ballad

Words and Music by Sammy Fain,
Herbert Magidson and Jack Yellen

Something to Live For

By Duke Ellington
and Billy Strayhorn

Speak Low

Medium

Words by Ogden Nash
Music by Kurt Weill

The Star-Crossed Lovers

By Duke Ellington
and Billy Strayhorn

Ballad

Stompin' at the Savoy

Medium

Words and Music by Benny Goodman, Edgar Sampson,
Chick Webb and Andy Razaf

Stormy Weather
(Keeps Rainin' All the Time)

Lyric by Ted Koehler
Music by Harold Arlen

Ballad

A String of Pearls

Words by Eddie DeLange
Music by Jerry Gray

Medium

Sunrise Serenade

Lyric by Jack Lawrence
Music by Frankie Carle

Medium

The Surrey with the Fringe on Top

Lyrics by Oscar Hammerstein II
Music by Richard Rodgers

Sweet and Lovely

Medium

Words and Music by Gus Arnheim,
Charles N. Daniels and Harry Tobias

Swinging on a Star

Words by Johnny Burke
Music by Jimmy Van Heusen

Take the "A" Train

Words and Music by
Billy Strayhorn

Tangerine

Medium

Words by Johnny Mercer
Music by Victor Schertzinger

Thanks for the Memory

Medium

Words and Music by Leo Robin
and Ralph Rainger

That Old Feeling

Medium

Words and Music by Lew Brown
and Sammy Fain

That Old Black Magic

Words by Johnny Mercer
Music by Harold Arlen

That Ole Devil Called Love

Ballad

By Doris Fisher
and Allan Roberts

Them There Eyes

Bright

Words and Music by Maceo Pinkard,
William Tracey and Doris Taubner

There Is No Greater Love

Medium

Words by Marty Symes
Music by Isham Jones

There Will Never Be Another You

Bright

Lyric by Mack Gordon
Music by Harry Warren

There's a Small Hotel

Words by Lorenz Hart
Music by Richard Rodgers

Medium

These Foolish Things
(Remind Me of You)

Words by Holt Marvell
Music by Jack Strachey and Harry Link

Ballad

Things Ain't What They Used to Be

By Mercer Ellington

Medium

Note: For solos use standard blues changes in B Flat (see "Blues Changes").

Thinking of You

Lyric by Bert Kalmar
Music by Harry Ruby

This Can't Be Love

Bright

Words by Lorenz Hart
Music by Richard Rodgers

This Love of Mine

Ballad or Medium

Words by Frank Sinatra
Music by Sol Parker and Henry Sanicola

This Year's Kisses

Ballad or Medium

Words and Music by
Irving Berlin

Tuxedo Junction

Words by Buddy Feyne
Music by Erskine Hawkins,
William Johnson and Julian Dash

Undecided

Words by Sid Robin
Music by Charlie Shavers

Bright

First you say you do and then you don't,___ and then you say you will and then you won't.___ You're
un-de-ci-ded now, so what are you gon-na do?_____

Now you want to play, and then it's no,___ and when you say you'll stay that's when you go.___ You're
un-de-ci-ded now, so what are you gon-na do?_____ I've been

sit-ting on a fence, and it does-n't make much sense, 'cause you keep me in sus-pense and you know it.___ Then you
prom-ise to re-turn, when you don't, I real-ly burn. Well, I guess I'll nev-er learn, and I show it.___

If you've got a heart and if you're kind,___ then don't keep us a-part. Make up your mind.___ You're
un-de-ci-ded now, so what are you gon-na do?_____

Until the Real Thing Comes Along

Ballad

Words and Music by
Mann Holiner, Alberta Nichols, Sammy Cahn,
Saul Chaplin and L.E. Freeman

Up with the Lark

Medium

Words and Music by
Jerome Kern

The Very Thought of You

Ballad

Words and Music by
Ray Noble

Violets for Your Furs

Ballad

By Tom Adair
and Matt Dennis

Wait till You See Her

Medium

Words by Lorenz Hart
Music by Richard Rodgers

What a Diff'rence a Day Made

Medium

Lyric by Stanley Adams
Music by Maria Grever

When You Wish upon a Star

Ballad

Words by Ned Washington
Music by Leigh Harline

Where or When

Words by Lorenz Hart
Music by Richard Rodgers

Medium

Who?

Lyrics by Otto Harbach and Oscar Hammerstein II
Music by Jerome Kern

Who Wouldn't Love You

Words by Bill Carey
Music by Carl Fischer

Medium

Why Can't I?

Medium

Words by Lorenz Hart
Music by Richard Rodgers

Why Don't You Do Right
(Get Me Some Money, Too!)

Medium

By Joe McCoy

Will You Still Be Mine

Bright

Words by Tom Adair
Music by Matt Dennis

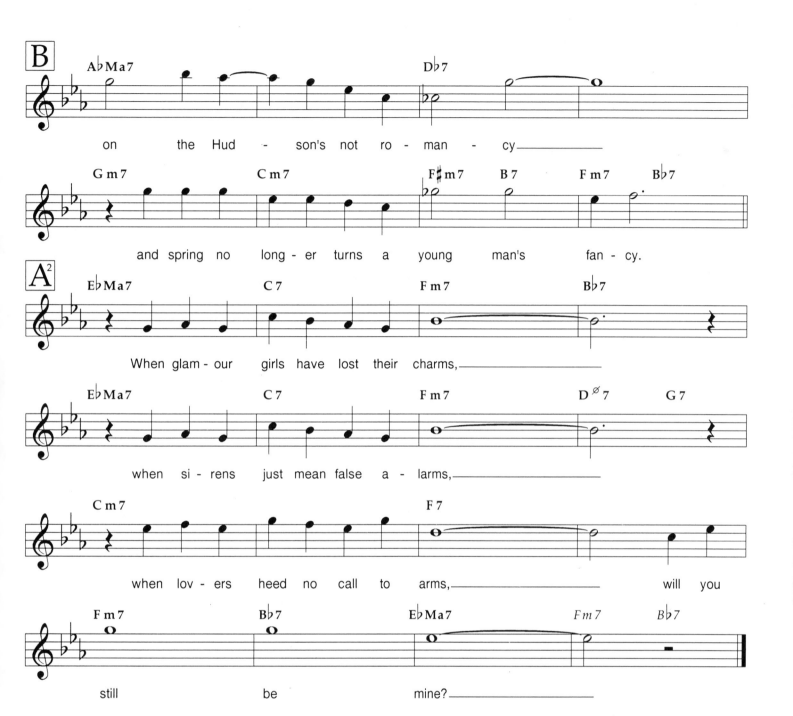

Wild Root

Bright

By Woody Herman
and Neal Hefti

Willow Weep for Me

Words and Music by
Ann Ronell

Yes Indeed

Medium

Words and Music by
Sy Oliver

You Don't Know What Love Is

Ballad

Words and Music by Don Raye
and Gene DePaul

MCA music publishing

You Turned the Tables on Me

Medium

Words by Sidney Mitchell
Music by Louis Alter

You'd Be So Nice to Come Home To

Bright

Words and Music by
Cole Porter

You're Blasé

Ballad

Words by Bruce Sievier
Music by Ord Hamilton

You're Easy to Dance With

Words and Music by
Irving Berlin

© Copyright 1942 by Irving Berlin
Copyright Renewed
International Copyright Secured   All Rights Reserved

You're Nearer

Ballad

Words by Lorenz Hart
Music by Richard Rodgers

200 OF THE BEST SONGS FROM

SWING ERA

BIOGRAPHIES

HAROLD ARLEN

Arlen combined a sophisticated harmonic sensibility with a blues tinge and created one of the greatest catalogs of songs in American music. He was born in 1905 in Buffalo, N.Y., and studied the piano as a boy. He quit high school to play music professionally. He joined The Buffalodians, a popular band that eventually went to New York. Arlen wrote arrangements for dance bands, worked in vaudeville, and eventually became Vincent Youmans' musical secretary. It was during this time that he wrote his first song, "Get Happy." It was such a huge hit that he was chosen, with his lyricist Ted Koehler, to write the score for the famous Cotton Club revues. Among the many songs written for these revues were "I've Got The World On A String" and "Stormy Weather." He also wrote several songs for Broadway revues, including "I've Gotta Right To Sing The Blues," "Ill Wind" and "Between The Devil And The Deep Blue Sea."

Moving to Hollywood, he collaborated with E.Y. Harburg on the score to *The Wizard Of Oz*, winning an Academy Award for "Over The Rainbow." His other songs from this period include "That Old Black Magic," "My Shining Hour," "One For My Baby," "Happiness Is A Thing Called Joe" and "This Time The Dream's On Me." Arlen returned to Broadway in 1944 and wrote two shows, *Bloomer Girl* and the magnificent *St. Louis Woman*.

The '50s brought such songs as "The Man That Got Away," "A Sleepin' Bee," "Push De Button" and "Goose Never Be A Peacock." He continued to write in the sixties, in particular with a young Martin Charnin as lyricist. He died in New York in 1986, one of the most beloved and admired songwriters in the show business community.

IRVING BERLIN

Jerome Kern was once asked what he felt Irving Berlin's place was in American music. Kern's reply was classic: "Irving Berlin has no place in American music. He **is** American music." It would be hard to disagree. Berlin's track record of song hits is amazing, and shows an incredible range. Show and movie songs, ballads, rhythm songs, up tempo jump tunes - Berlin wrote them all.

Israel Baline was born in Russia in 1888 and came to the United States at the age of five. His father died when he was thrirteen, and the boy went to work in Bowery saloons a year later, often as a singing waiter. While he was working at once such joint, The Pelham Cafe, he wrote the lyrics to his first published song, "Marie From Sunny Italy." He wrote his first hit, "Sadie Salome, Go Home" in 1908. But his first worldwide smash hit was "Alexander's Ragtime Band" which he wrote in 1911. This was followed by "Everybody's Doin' It," a song describing the new dance sensation in America, the Turkey Trot.

Berlin eventually became his own publisher, and published not only his own songs, but the songs of the top Broadway and Hollywood composers. His list of song hits through the years would fill a number of pages, but some of the biggest were "Always," "Blue Skies," "Change Partners," "Easter Parade," "God Bless America," "I Love A Piano," "Lazy," "Let Yourself Go," Say It Isn't So" and "White Christmas." Berlin lived to the incredible age of 101.

MATT DENNIS

Dennis not only made his mark as a songwriter, but as a television and nightclub performer as well. He was born in 1914 and led a band while he was still in school. He sang with the Horace Heidt orchestra, and put together a band which was fronted by future singing star Dick Haymes. While Dennis was performing in a club in Hollywood, lyricist Tom Adair came in, liked what he heard and asked Dennis to write some songs with him. "Will You Still Be Mine?," "Let's Get Away From It All" and "Everything Happens To Me" were all written in a week. Jo Stafford, who was singing with The Pied Pipers in Tommy Dorsey's band, had the songwriting team play them for Tommy. He not only published them all, he hired the team to write material exclusively for the Dorsey organization.

After military service, Dennis appeared in supper clubs in Hollywood and New York, and even had one of the earliest weekly television shows to be broadcast in color. Around this time, he also composed one of the finest saloon songs ever written, "Angel Eyes." At this writing, Dennis is still writing songs, and has published piano arrangements of jazz standards for Sheet Music Magazine.

HOWARD DIETZ

Dietz maintained a full-time job as chief of publicity and advertising at MGM while collaborating with composer Arthur Schwartz. He was born in New York City in 1896. Like his future colleagues Lorenz Hart and Oscar Hammerstein, he attended Columbia University and contributed to the college's publications.

He went into advertising after serving in World War I, and MGM's trademark lion was his creation. In the same year, 1924, he contributed the lyrics to the show *Dear Sir* with music by Jerome Kern. His most enduring collaboration started with a letter from a lawyer; Arthur Schwartz wanted to leave his practice and write songs with Dietz. Dietz wrote back saying Schwartz needed more experience. Five years later, they wrote their first song, "Hammacher Schlemmer, I Love You," and one of the great songwriting teams was born. Some of their many hits were "Dancing In The Dark," Alone Together," "A Shine On Your Shoes," "That's Entertainment," "By Myself," "Triplets" and "I Guess I'll Have To Change My Plan."

He also wrote english lyrics to the Johann Strauss operetta "Die Fledermaus," performed at the Metropolitan Opera in 1949. In the '60s, he collaborated with Schwartz again on the shows "The Gay Life" and "Jennie." He was stricken with Parkinson's Disease, and was one of the first to try the drug L-Dopa, which improved his condition considerably. He died in 1983.

DUKE ELLINGTON

One of the greatest composers of this century, Ellington is credited with writing over 2,000 compositions, many of them songs, most of them for his own orchestra. He was born in Washington, D.C. in 1899, was a gifted graphic artist and athlete, but was playing piano professionally while he was still a teenager. He came to New York in 1924, and his first big break came when his small ensemble was chosen to play at the Kentucky Club. Radio broadcasts and recordings made the band known, but it became a national attraction when music publisher and manager Irving Mills took over the management of the band. The Duke Ellington Orchestra was soon playing at New York's chic night club, The Cotton Club, and appearing in motion pictures. Among Ellington's earliest successes were "East St. Louis Toodle-oo," "Mood Indigo" and "Sophisticated Lady." Ellington toured Europe in 1932 and was lionized by fans, critics and even British royalty.

In 1939, he and Mills severed their relationship, and Duke entered one of the most creative periods of his career. His 1940 ensemble is regarded as perhaps the best band he ever led, and one of the great ensembles of the swing era. Such compositions as "Jack The Bear," "Harlem Airshaft," "C-Jam Blues," "I've Got It Bad" and "Cottontail" come from this period. He first played Carnegie Hall in 1943, premiering a fifty minute concert work, *Black, Brown and Beige*. It was the first of many Ellington concerts at Carnegie, and Ellington usually wrote a new piece for the occasion.

When the big band era ended in the late '40s, Ellington kept his on the road, but he was losing many of his long-time band members, and the next few years were difficult for him. He bounced back suddenly in 1956 when he stopped the show at the Newport Jazz Festival, resulting in a Time Magazine front cover, and renewed interest in the band. Until his death in 1974, he toured, recorded prolifically, and continued to compose music for his band, and large concert works and ballets for ensembles throughout the world. He was the recipient of many honorary doctorates, citations and awards throughout his life. His orchestra continues to perform and record.

OSCAR HAMMERSTEIN II

Hammerstein is perhaps best known for his collaborations with Richard Rodgers, but he wrote several hit productions before he and Rodgers became a team, in particular the classic musical *Showboat*. Hammerstein was born in New York in 1895. His grandfather had created and managed the Manhattan Opera House, which was a formidable rival to the Metropolitan Opera. His uncle was a successful producer, and his father was the manager of the Victoria Theatre. Oscar studied law at Columbia and obtained a degree, but his real interest was in writing the college varsity shows, some of which he directed.

His first Broadway production as librettist/lyricist was *Always You* in 1920. He worked frequently with composer Herbert Stothart in those early years. In 1924, he wrote his first big hit production *Rose-Marie* which is still a popular show in amateur and stock companies. His first collaboration with Jerome Kern was the hit musical *Sunny* in 1925. Their groundbreaking theatre work *Showboat* premiered in 1927. They also wrote *Sweet Adeline* for Helen Morgan in 1929, and *Music In The Air* in 1932.

For the next several years, Hammerstein wrote a series of shows that were unsuccessful, and several Broadway insiders wondered whether he had lost his touch. He bounced back when Richard Rodgers needed a new collaborator in 1942, and the innovative *Oklahoma* was the result. This was soon followed by *Carousel, South Pacific, The King and I, Flower Drum Song* and *The Sound Of Music*. Hammerstein died in 1960 of cancer. His legacy lives on in the many revivals of his shows, and in particular, the work of his protege, Stephen Sondheim.

E.Y. 'YIP' HARBURG

Harburg's most successful song was written in 1939 for Judy Garland. It was almost removed from the film *The Wizard Of Oz*, but producer Arthur Freed fought for it, and "Over The Rainbow" won the Academy Award for best song that year. Harburg was born in New York in 1896. He wrote verse in high school, and as a student at City College of New York, co-wrote a column with future lyricist Ira Gershwin. He went into the electrical supply business after graduation, but the Depression forced the business to close. Harburg considered this the break of his life. He called Ira Gershwin, who introduced him to composer Jay Gorney. They collaborated on "Brother, Can You Spare A Dime" which appeared in the Broadway revue *Americana*. They went on to write for *Earl Carroll's Vanities*, and later wrote Bob Hope's first Broadway show, *Ballyhoo*. The songs "What Is There To Say," "I Like the Likes Of You" and "April In Paris" established Harburg on Broadway.

Like many of his fellow songwriters, Harburg went to Hollywood in the late '30s and wrote songs for the movies. *The Wizard Of Oz* gave Harburg the opportunity to write a score with old friend Harold Arlen. He subsequently contributed many classic songs for MGM movies, such as "Lydia The Tattooed Lady" and "Happiness Is A Thing Called Joe." When he returned to Broadway in 1944, he wrote the book and lyrics for the show *Bloomer Girl*. By now, the subject matter of Harburg's projects became more and more political; some critics felt he was too controversial. His show *Finian's Rainbow* reflected his beliefs about prejudice. It was a huge hit, but waited over twenty years for a film version. *Flahooley* also had a wonderful score written with Sammy Fain, but was a flop. Harburg did not write another show until 1957, a hit entitled *Jamaica* starring Lena Horne and Ricardo Montalban.

In the '60s and '70s, Harburg performed at colleges and on television, singing his songs from Broadway and Hollywood. His last song was the poignant "Time, You Old Gypsy Man." He passed away in 1981.

JEROME KERN

Before Kern, the Broadway musical was a European product, with American entries being mostly frivolous excuses for singing and dancing. With their pioneering musicals for the Princess Theatre, Kern, Guy Bolton and P.G. Wodehouse revolutionized the musical. The shows they created had intelligent books, stories that related to American life and songs that helped to advance the plot of the show rather than an excuse for the star to sing. These innovations culminated in the revolutionary *Showboat*, still one of the greatest Broadway musicals of all time.

Kern was born in 1885. He studied piano with his mother, and saw his first Broadway show at the age of ten. He knew immediately he wanted to be a composer for the stage. He enrolled at the New York College Of Music in 1902. He also met Max Dreyfus, head of T. B. Harms. Dreyfus took a liking to Kern, and helped him interpolate his songs into British imports currently playing on Broadway. Even though his song "How'd You Like To Spoon With Me" was very popular, Kern's breakthrough song was the beautiful "They Didn't Believe Me." The Princess Theatre shows followed, which made him the most popular new composer on Broadway. Several shows with various collaborators were written in the early '20s; *Sally*, *Sunny* and *Sitting Pretty*.

In the '30s, after the success of *Showboat*, Kern was active in Hollywood and Broadway. He wrote many of his greatest songs during this period, such as "Smoke Gets In Your Eyes," "Yesterdays," "I Won't Dance," "Pick Yourself Up" and "The Folks Who Live On the Hill." In 1939, Kern wrote his last score for Broadway with Oscar Hammerstein, *Very Warm for May*. Although the show only ran fifty-nine performances, it featured what many say was Kern's finest achievement, the song "All The Things You Are." Kern returned to Hollywood and continued writing songs for movies; "Remind Me," "Dearly Beloved," and another masterpiece, "Long Ago (And Far Away)" were some of the titles. He was working on a revival of *Showboat* when he died suddenly in New York in 1945.

BURTON LANE

Lane's career has resulted in many standard songs written for Broadway and Hollywood. He was born in New York in 1912, and left school at fifteen to become a song plugger at Remick Music. He contributed to the show *Artists And Models* when he was eighteen years old, and despite the show's failure, his songs were heard and applauded by George Gershwin. Howard Dietz also became a fan, and added two Burton Lane songs to his revue *Three's A Crowd*.

Broadway was presenting fewer musicals during the early years of the Depression. Lane went to Hollywood at this time, where he wrote his first big hit, "Everything I Have Is Yours." Other songs written during his early Hollywood years were "Says My Heart," "The Lady's In Love With You," "I Hear Music," "Dancing On A Dime" and "How About You." In 1947, Lane co-wrote *Finian's Rainbow* with 'Yip' Harburg, and such songs as "Old Devil Moon," "How Are Things In Glocca Morra" and "If This Isn't Love" became standards.

Back in Hollywood in 1951, Lane wrote one of his greatest songs, "Too Late Now" for the movie *Royal Wedding*. In 1965, he wrote an excellent score for the show *On A Clear Day You Can See Forever*, which included the title song, "Come Back To Me" and "She Wasn't You." Lane's last Broadway show was *Carmelina*, produced in 1979. Although the show was a flop, Lane's music received excellent reviews. Lane's last project was a score for the animated musical *Heidi's Song*.

FRANK LOESSER

Loesser was a successful lyricist in Hollywood before he was given the opportunity to write both words and music for the show *Where's Charley?* The show became one of the biggest hits of the season. He was born in New York in 1910. He started writing song lyrics in his late teens; a song he wrote in 1934, "Junk Man," was recorded by Benny Goodman.

In 1936, he signed his first Hollywood contract to be a staff lyricist for Universal Pictures. In 1937, he moved over to Paramount, where he would remain until 1949. His songs from his Hollywood years include "The Moon Of Manakoora," "Small Fry," Two Sleepy People," "Heart And Soul," "I Don't Want To Walk Without You," "They're Either Too Young Or Too Old" and "Spring Will Be A Little Late This Year." He wrote both the words and music for the wartime hit, "Praise The Lord And Pass The Ammunition."

In 1948, he wrote both words and music for an entire score for producers Cy Feuer and Ernie Martin. *Where's Charley* was a huge hit, and their next show together, *Guys and Dolls*, was an even bigger one. Loesser followed this with *The Most Happy Fella*. Although a success when it was first on Broadway, the show really did not catch on; it's reputation has grown in stature since its premiere in 1956, with several major productions in the '70s and '80s. Loesser's next production was *Greenwillow* which has one of his loveliest scores. *How To Succeed In Business Without Really Trying* was his next show, and it was his last smash hit. Loesser died in 1969.

JIMMY McHUGH

McHugh had a long and varied career as composer for Broadway and motion pictures. He was born in Boston in 1895. While he was studying at Staley College in Boston, he worked for the Boston Opera House. He was offered a scholarship to the New England Conservatory Of Music, but turned it down to become a song plugger at the Boston office of Irving Berlin's publishing operation.

He moved to New York and joined the publishing firm of Mills Music, where he soon became one of the office managers. In 1922, he contributed his first songs to the Cotton Club revues, eventually collaborating on nine editions. Some of those songs include "When My Sugar Walks Down The Street" and "I Can't Believe That You're In Love With Me." In 1927, he met Dorothy Fields. Together, they wrote such hits as "I Can't Give You Anything But Love, Baby," "On The Sunny Side Of The Street," "Diga Diga Doo," "Don't Blame Me" and "Exactly Like You." In 1930, the team moved to Hollywood and wrote "I'm In The Mood For Love" and "I Feel A Song Comin' On."

When Fields moved back to Broadway in 1935, McHugh teamed up with Ted Koehler, writing "I'm Shooting High" and with Harold Adamson, "Where Are You?" and "My Own." He free-lanced in Hollywood throughout the '40s; the songs "The Music Stopped," "Here Comes Heaven Again" and "A Lovely Way To Spend An Evening" were written during this period. He was nominated for an Academy Award five times for best song, but never won.

In the '50s McHugh put together a nightclub act that toured the U.S. and appeared on television. His final years were spent doing charity work and serving as vice-president of ASCAP. He died in Beverly HIlls in 1969.

JOHNNY MERCER

Mercer has been called one of the greatest all-around lyricists in American popular song. Certainly no one has shown the wide range and brilliance in lyric writing as Mercer has, whether it is a ballad, rhythm song, country song or even an art song like "On The Nodaway Road."

Mercer was born in Savannah, Georgia in 1909. He became a member of the Paul Whiteman orchestra as vocalist and lyricist, writing such songs as "Pardon My Southern Accent." After leaving Whiteman, Hollywood beckoned, and such songs as "You Must Have Been A Beautiful Baby," "Hooray For Hollywood," "Too Marvelous For Words" and "Jeepers Creepers" were the result. He even wrote his own music for the song "You Grow Sweeter (As The Years Go By)."

In the 1940s, Mercer collaborated with Jerome Kern, Hoagy Carmichael and Harold Arlen. "Skylark," "I Remember You," "Tangerine," "I'm Old Fashioned," "Laura," "Dearly Beloved" and "Hit The Road To Dreamland" were some of his biggest hits during this period. Even a difficult song such as "Blues In The Night" became a huge hit, much to the surprise of Mercer and Arlen, who thought that the song was too complex to catch on. The team also composed a landmark score for an unsuccessful Broadway show, *St. Louis Woman*, which included the classic "Come Rain Or Come Shine." Mercer was an original partner in the Capitol Record Company, and signed such artists as Jo Stafford, Stan Kenton, Nat 'King' Cole, The Pied Pipers, Peggy Lee and Margaret Whiting to make recordings. It became the most successful post-war record label in the music business.

The '50s and '60s brought more successes such as "When The World Was Young," "Emily," "Autumn Leaves" and two songs that won Academy Awards: "Moon River" and "Days Of Wine And Roses," both with music by Henry Mancini. Mercer passed away in 1976.

COLE PORTER

Porter was one of the most sophisticated songwriters in American music, and his witty songs still surprise and even shock modern audiences. He was born in Peru, Indiana in 1893. At his family's insistence that he become a lawyer, Cole attended Yale University. But music was what he was interested in, eventually studying classical music in France. His first Broadway show, *See America First*, was a failure. Until the late '20s, except for an occasional song, Porter stayed away from Broadway.

It was Irving Berlin who encouraged him to return to the theatre full time. His first hit show, *Paris*, featured the showstopper, "Let's Do It (Let's Fall In Love)." His next show included "You Do Something To Me." Later shows yielded such hits as "Begin The Beguine," "Night And Day," "I Get A Kick Out Of You," "Anything Goes," It's De-lovely" and "Ridin' High."

In 1937, Porter's legs were crushed in a riding accident. Against the advice of doctors, he refused to have his legs amputated. He was in pain for the rest of his life, but continued to write song hits for motion pictures and Broadway. Songs from the '40s and '50s include "You'd Be So Nice To Come Home To," "Dream Dancing," "Be A Clown," So In Love," "Wunderbar," "I Love Paris," "I Love You" and "All Of You." His last project was a television musical called *Aladdin*.

In the last years of his life, he witnessed major recorded retrospectives of his songs by such artists as Fred Astaire and Ella Fitzgerald. He died in California in 1964.

RALPH RAINGER

Although not as recognized as many other hit songwriters, Ralph Rainger was one of the most talented songwriters in Hollywood in the 1930s. He was born Ralph Reichenthal in New York in 1901, and studied to be a lawyer. After he graduated, he was the pit pianist for the Broadway show *Queen High*. He became part of a duo-piano vaudeville team with Edgar 'Cookie' Fairchild. (Fairchild later became a conductor/musical director on radio.) Rainger wrote his first song in 1929 when a bluesy number was needed for *The Little Show*, in which Rainger was rehearsal pianist. The song "Moanin' Low," with lyrics by Howard Dietz, was a big hit.

Rainger joined the songwriting staff of Paramount Pictures in 1930, collaborating with Leo Robin. They became the first resident songwriters for Bing Crosby, and wrote many hits for him, including "Please," Love In Bloom," "June In January," "Blue Hawaii," "Thanks For The Memory" and "Sweet Is The Word For You." With Dorothy Parker he wrote "I Wished On The Moon." Rainger also composed a number of novelty and instrumental pieces, including the music to an experimental animated short subject by Oscar Fischinger, "Allegretto." This fascinating short has become a great favorite at film festivals. Rainger died in a plane crash in California in 1942.

LEO ROBIN

Robin's collaboration with Ralph Rainger created many popular songs. However, he went on to write many more standards with Jerome Kern, Sigmund Romberg, Harold Arlen and Jule Styne. He was born in 1900 in Pittsburgh, Pennsylvania. He came to New York in the late '20s intending to write plays. He met playwright George S. Kaufman, who was more impressed with the young man's lyrics than his plays.

By 1928, Robin collaborated with Vincent Youmans and Clifford Grey on the hit, "Hallelujah!" In the same year, publisher Max Dreyfus sent him to Hollywood to write songs with Richard Whiting. The first wave of movie musicals was in full swing, and Robin and Whiting wrote such songs as "Louise," and Beyond The Blue Horizon." His collaboration with Ralph Rainger brought him an Academy Award for the song, "Thanks For The Memory" in 1938. With Jerome Kern, he wrote the score for the movie *Centennial Summer*, which included "In Love In Vain" and "Up With The Lark." His collaboration with Harold Arlen created the songs "What's Good About Goodbye?" and "Hooray For Love." He wrote the score for the Broadway show *Gentlemen Prefer Blondes* with Jule Styne, and "Diamonds Are A Girl's Best Friend" and "Bye, Bye Baby" resulted. Robin continued to write scores for the movies until he retired in the 1960s. He died in 1984.

RODGERS AND HART

A team for over twenty years, Richard Rodgers and Lorenz Hart were responsible for some of the most innovative shows of the '20s and '30s. Both were born in New York, Rodgers in 1902, Hart in 1895. Both became enamored with the musical theatre when they were young. They met in 1918, and soon after that initial meeting, they were to write fifteen songs in a short period. One of them, "Any Old Place With You" was interpolated into a Broadway show produced by veteran producer Lew Fields. But the next few years were disheartening for the team, who wrote a number of college and amateur shows while waiting for a break. They got that break in 1925, when the *Garrick Gaieties*, a benefit that was to have two performances, actually became a full-fledged Broadway production running 161 performances.

Until 1931, there were many Rodgers and Hart shows on Broadway, with such songs as "The Blue Room," "Mountain Greenery," "My Heart Stood Still," "You Took Advantage Of Me" "and "Ten Cents A Dance." They received an offer from Hollywood and worked on a number of motion pictures for the next few years. Many of their songs were not used, but such classics as "Isn't It Romantic," "Lover," "It's Easy To Remember" and "Blue Moon" were heard, published and recorded. Back on Broadway in 1935, the team wrote the score and story for *On Your Toes*, which was the first of many innovative musicals they worked on. *Pal Joey*, for instance, was a controversial show when it opened, and even though it was popular, it's true importance was only realized when it was revived in 1952. "I Could Write A Book" and "Bewitched" were written for the show.

Hart, who'd always been difficult to work with, became downright erratic by 1942. He turned down the show that later became *Oklahoma*, and realized that the team of Rodgers and Hammerstein was too good to only write one show together. Hart worked on one more show with Rodgers, a revival of *A Connecticut Yankee*, and died of pneumonia soon afterwards. Rodgers, of course went on to write several hit shows with Hammerstein, and later collaborated with Stephen Sondheim on one show. He was still writing music (and sometimes lyrics) for new projects until his death in 1979.

SIGMUND ROMBERG

One of the great composers of American operetta, Romberg was born in Hungary in 1887. He came to the U.S. in 1909 and led dance orchestras in restaurants for a number of years in New York. His first compositions were published in 1913.

In 1914, Romberg became a staff composer for the Schubert Brothers, a theatre empire that owned many theatres and presented shows all across the country. Romberg's first show for the Schuberts was *The Whirl Of The World*. Fifteen shows later, he composed the score to *Maytime*, his first hit. His show *Blossom Time* was so popular that road companies were performing the show for over thirty years. *The Student Prince* was the first of a series of successful operettas that had music by Romberg. Other popular productions were *The Desert Song* and *The New Moon*. These shows contained such songs as "Serenade," "Deep In My Heart, Dear," "One Alone," "Softly As In A Morning Sunrise," "Wanting You," "Lover, Come Back To Me" and "Stouthearted Men."

He wrote many other songs long after the operetta boom ended, particularly "Close As Pages In A Book." In the late '40s, Romberg toured the country conducting concerts of his classic songs, as well as making recordings. He died in New York in 1951.

ARTHUR SCHWARTZ

A successful lawyer, Schwartz wrote songs in his spare time until his collaboration with lyricist Howard Dietz became so fruitful that he gave up his practice and never looked back. Born in New York in 1900, Schwartz wrote songs as a teenager with lyricist Lorenz Hart for summer camp shows. It was Hart who encouraged Schwartz to make music his full time occupation.

With Howard Dietz, Schwartz wrote such classic songs as "Alone Together," "Something To Remember You By," "The Moment I Saw You," "Dancing In The Dark," "You And The Night And The Music" and "I See Your Face Before Me." Schwartz moved to California and not only wrote songs, but produced motion pictures as well. In 1951, Schwartz wrote the score to the Broadway musical *A Tree Grows In Brooklyn* with Dorothy Fields. In 1953, MGM produced a motion picture called *The Band Wagon*, which had a Howard Dietz-Arthur Schwartz score made up of many of their older hits, plus a new song, "That's Entertainment." Schwartz was back on Broadway with the show *By The Beautiful Sea* in 1954, which included the classic song, "Alone Too Long." In the late '60s, Schwartz worked on a musical adaptation of *Nicholas Nickelby* while he was living in England. He died in 1984.

JAMES VAN HEUSEN

Born Edward Chester Babcock in 1913, Jimmy Van Heusen's two main collaborators were Johnny Burke and Sammy Cahn. With both men, he wrote a series of hits which became standards.

Babcock changed his name to Van Heusen in honor of the shirt company. While studying music at Syracuse University, Van Heusen met Harold Arlen's brother Jerry, and it was through his introduction to Harold that Van Heusen wrote songs for the famous Cotton Club in New York. Van Heusen was a song plugger at Remick's music publishing company when he started writing songs with bandleader/songwriter Eddie DeLange. Two of their songs were "Deep In A Dream" and "Heaven Can Wait."

Van Heusen signed a contract with Paramount Pictures in 1940, where he began his collaboration with Johnny Burke. Together, they became Bing Crosby's songwriting team, writing many hits for 'The Groaner,' including "Moonlight Becomes You," "Sunday, Monday Or Always," "It's Always You," "It Could Happen To You," "Like Someone In Love" and "Swinging On A Star." Burke and Van Heusen wrote a Broadway show in 1953 called *Carnival In Flanders*, which yielded the great standard "Here's That Rainy Day."

Burke fell ill in 1954, and Van Heusen started a new partnership with Sammy Cahn. Frank Sinatra called them his favorite songwriters, and the hits "The Tender Trap," "All The Way," "Come Dance With Me," Come Fly With Me," "Love and Marriage" and "All My Tomorrows" were written for him. In addition, Van Heusen served as Sinatra's vocal coach and occasional piano/conductor. Van Heusen died in California in 1990.

VICTOR YOUNG

Victor Young did it all; composer, arranger, conductor, producer and supervisor for recording companies, film companies and many stars. He was a pioneer in the art of music for film, and he made hundreds of recordings conducting every type of music imaginable. He was also a composer of many hit songs, truly one of the great musical talents in America.

He was born in Chicago in 1900 and started playing the violin when he was a boy. He studied the instrument in Poland, and returned to the U.S. in 1920, intending to become a concert violinist. But by 1922, he was the concertmaster for the Million Dollar Theatre in Los Angeles, one of the legendary movie palaces that featured a large orchestra to accompany motion pictures.

In 1929, he made his first radio broadcast, and two years later, he became the musical director of Brunswick Records, supervising and arranging and/or conducting many of their recordings. In 1935, he joined the staff of the Decca Record Company, where he would remain as arranger/conductor until his death. In the same year, he was also hired by Paramount Pictures to compose music for films. Among his many scores were *For Whom The Bell Tolls*, *The Uninvited* (which featured his song "Stella By Starlight"), *The Blue Dahlia*, *Samson And Delilah*, *The Quiet Man*, and *Around The World In Eighty Days*. The last-named score brought Young an Academy Award. Some of his biggest hit songs included "A Hundred Years From Today," "Beautiful Love," "Sweet Sue - Just You," "A Ghost Of A Chance," "When I Fall In Love" and "My Foolish Heart." Young died in 1956, leaving a great legacy of music behind him.

ARTIST INDEX

CANNONBALL ADDERLEY I REMEMBER YOU

THIS CAN'T BE LOVE

DAVID ALLYN IT NEVER ENTERED MY MIND

WAIT TILL YOU SEE HER

GENE AMMONS LONG AGO (AND FAR AWAY)

TANGERINE

LOUIS ARMSTRONG IT'S BEEN A LONG, LONG TIME

FRED ASTAIRE BY MYSELF

CHEEK TO CHEEK

I'M OLD FASHIONED

MY SHINING HOUR

THINKING OF YOU

MILDRED BAILEY DARN THAT DREAM

MY LAST AFFAIR

THANKS FOR THE MEMORY

CHET BAKER DON'T EXPLAIN

LET'S GET LOST

THAT OLE DEVIL CALLED LOVE

COUNT BASIE APRIL IN PARIS

BLUE AND SENTIMENTAL

BROADWAY

CHEROKEE (INDIAN LOVE SONG)

GEORGE BENSON (I'M AFRAID) THE MASQUERADE IS OVER

TUXEDO JUNCTION

BUNNY BERIGAN I CAN'T GET STARTED WITH YOU

CONNEE BOSWELL THE NEARNESS OF YOU

CLIFFORD BROWN EASY LIVING

GONE WITH THE WIND

WHERE OR WHEN

LES BROWN SENTIMENTAL JOURNEY

KENNY BURRELL YOU TURNED THE TABLES ON ME

BETTY CARTER HEART AND SOUL

RON CARTER YES INDEED

JUNE CHRISTY EASY STREET

I'LL TAKE ROMANCE

WILLOW WEEP FOR ME

BUDDY CLARK HOW ARE THINGS IN GLOCCA MORRA

LARRY CLINTON HEART AND SOUL

(I'M AFRAID) THE MASQUERADE IS OVE

NAT KING COLE
(KING COLE TRIO) CANDY

A HANDFUL OF STARS

IS YOU IS, OR IS YOU AIN'T (MA' BABY)

JOHN COLTRANE ALL OR NOTHING AT ALL

DON'T TAKE YOUR LOVE FROM ME

EV'RY TIME WE SAY GOODBYE

I LOVE YOU

I SEE YOUR FACE BEFORE ME

I'M OLD FASHIONED

LIKE SOMEONE IN LOVE

MY SHINING HOUR

THE NIGHT WE CALLED IT A DAY

OUT OF THIS WORLD

RUSSIAN LULLABY

SAY IT (OVER AND OVER AGAIN)

YOU DON'T KNOW WHAT LOVE IS

BING CROSBY AREN'T YOU GLAD YOU'RE YOU

FELLA WITH AN UMBRELLA

I WISH I WERE IN LOVE AGAIN

JUNE IN JANUARY

LIKE SOMEONE IN LOVE

OUT OF THIS WORLD

PENNIES FROM HEAVEN

RUSSIAN LULLABY

SWINGING ON A STAR

THAT OLD BLACK MAGIC

THE VERY THOUGHT OF YOU

MILES DAVIS

DARN THAT DREAM

I COULD WRITE A BOOK

IT'S ONLY A PAPER MOON

IT COULD HAPPEN TO YOU

MY FUNNY VALENTINE

MY SHIP

SOMETHING I DREAMED LAST NIGHT

THE SURREY WITH THE FRINGE ON TOP

THERE IS NO GREATER LOVE

PAUL DESMOND

BEWITCHED

POLKA DOTS AND MOONBEAMS

KENNY DORHAM

GOLDEN EARRINGS

IT MIGHT AS WELL BE SPRING

JIMMY DORSEY

I DIDN'T KNOW WHAT TIME IT WAS

I HEAR A RHAPSODY

I'M GLAD THERE IS YOU
(IN THIS WORLD OF ORDINARY PEOPLE)

TANGERINE

TOMMY DORSEY

ALL THE THINGS YOU ARE

EVERYTHING HAPPENS TO ME

I CONCENTRATE ON YOU

I'LL NEVER SMILE AGAIN

IMAGINATION

IN THE BLUE OF EVENING

THE LADY IS A TRAMP

LET'S GET AWAY FROM IT ALL

MARIE

THE NIGHT WE CALLED IT A DAY

POLKA DOTS AND MOONBEAMS

THIS LOVE OF MINE

WHO?

WILL YOU STILL BE MINE

YES INDEED

EDDY DUCHIN

I COULD WRITE A BOOK

BILLY ECKSTINE

SKYLARK

CLIFF EDWARDS

WHEN YOU WISH UPON A STAR

DUKE ELLINGTON

CARAVAN

CHELSEA BRIDGE

COME SUNDAY

DON'T GET AROUND MUCH ANYMORE

DON'T YOU KNOW I CARE
(OR DON'T YOU CARE TO KNOW)

EVERYTHING BUT YOU

FLAMINGO

I GOT IT BAD AND THAT AIN'T GOOD

I LET A SONG GO OUT OF MY HEART

I'M BEGINNING TO SEE THE LIGHT

I'M JUST A LUCKY SO AND SO

IN A SENTIMENTAL MOOD

JOHNNY COME LATELY

PRELUDE TO A KISS

RAIN CHECK

SOMETHING TO LIVE FOR

THE STAR-CROSSED LOVERS

TAKE THE 'A' TRAIN

THINGS AIN'T WHAT THEY USED TO BE

BILL EVANS

EV'RYTHING I LOVE

I HEAR A RHAPSODY

I SHOULD CARE

I'VE GOT YOU UNDER MY SKIN

SOMEDAY MY PRINCE WILL COME

UP WITH THE LARK

WHEN YOU WISH UPON A STAR

ART FARMER

BY MYSELF

JUNE IN JANUARY

RAIN CHECK

SHEP FIELDS

THAT OLD FEELING

ELLA FITZGERALD

BETWEEN THE DEVIL AND
THE DEEP BLUE SEA

A FINE ROMANCE

FOR YOU, FOR ME, FOR EVERMORE

I WISH I WERE IN LOVE AGAIN

I'VE GOT MY LOVE TO KEEP ME WARM

IT'S ONLY A PAPER MOON

JERSEY BOUNCE

244

THE LADY IS A TRAMP

MOONLIGHT IN VERMONT

MY LAST AFFAIR

RIDIN' HIGH

STOMPIN' AT THE SAVOY

THAT OLD BLACK MAGIC

THEM THERE EYES

THESE FOOLISH THINGS
(REMIND ME OF YOU)

WHY DON'T YOU DO RIGHT
(GET ME SOME MONEY TOO!)

YOU'D BE SO NICE TO COME TO

TOMMY FLANAGAN   NO MORE

THE VERY THOUGHT OF YOU

JUDY GARLAND   FOR YOU, FOR ME, FOR EVERMORE

STAN GETZ   I'M GLAD THERE IS YOU
(IN THIS WORLD OF ORDINARY PEOPLE)

SENTIMENTAL JOURNEY

SKYLARK

THANKS FOR THE MEMORY

YOU'RE BLASÉ

DIZZY GILLESPIE   FLAMINGO

TAKE THE 'A' TRAIN

BENNY GOODMAN   AIR MAIL SPECIAL

BETWEEN THE DEVIL AND
THE DEEP BLUE SEA

CLOSE AS PAGES IN A BOOK

GOOD-BYE

I'VE FOUND A NEW BABY
(A/K/A I FOUND A NEW BABY)

IN THE BLUE OF EVENING

JERSEY BOUNCE

THE LADY'S IN LOVE WITH YOU

RIDIN' HIGH

STOMPIN' AT THE SAVOY

THERE'S A SMALL HOTEL

UNDECIDED

YOU TURNED THE TABLES ON ME

DEXTER GORDON   BROADWAY

A NIGHTINGALE SANG
IN BERKELEY SQUARE

GLEN GRAY

COLEMAN HAWKINS

ERSKINE HAWKINS

DICK HAYMES

WOODY HERMAN

HILDEGARDE

BILLIE HOLIDAY

WILLOW WEEP FOR ME

DON'T TAKE YOUR LOVE FROM ME

I SEE YOUR FACE BEFORE ME

IT'S A BLUE WORLD

TUXEDO JUNCTION

FOR YOU, FOR ME, FOR EVERMORE

I JUST FOUND OUT ABOUT LOVE

IT MIGHT AS WELL BE SPRING

BIJOU

BLUE FLAME

DOCTOR JAZZ

DOWN UNDER

SWEET AND LOVELY

THERE WILL NEVER BE ANOTHER YOU

WILD ROOT

THE LAST TIME I SAW PARIS

CHEEK TO CHEEK

DON'T EXPLAIN

EASY LIVING

FINE AND MELLOW

A FINE ROMANCE

FOOLIN' MYSELF

GOD BLESS THE CHILD

I GOTTA RIGHT TO SING THE BLUES

I HADN'T ANYONE TILL YOU

I'LL BE AROUND

I'LL BE SEEING YOU

I'VE GOT MY LOVE TO KEEP ME WARM

LOVER MAN (OH, WHERE CAN YOU BE?

NO MORE

PRELUDE TO A KISS

THAT OLE DEVIL CALLED LOVE

THEM THERE EYES

THESE FOOLISH THINGS
(REMIND ME OF YOU)

THIS YEAR'S KISSES

UNTIL THE REAL THING COMES ALONG

VIOLETS FOR YOUR FURS

YOU DON'T KNOW WHAT LOVE IS

SHIRLEY HORN	I JUST FOUND OUT ABOUT LOVE	**ETHEL MERMAN**	LET'S HAVE ANOTHER CUP O' COFFEE
LENA HORNE	RIGHT AS THE RAIN	**GLENN MILLER**	APRIL IN PARIS
FREDDIE HUBBARD	FULL MOON AND EMPTY ARMS		A HANDFUL OF STARS
AHMAD JAMAL	POINCIANA (SONG OF THE TREE)		I'LL BE AROUND
HARRY JAMES	I'M BEGINNING TO SEE THE LIGHT		IN THE MOOD
	I'VE HEARD THAT SONG BEFORE		A LOVELY WAY TO SPEND AN EVENING
	IT'S BEEN A LONG, LONG TIME		MOONLIGHT BECOMES YOU
	MY SILENT LOVE		A NIGHTINGALE SANG IN BERKELEY SQUARE
	A SINNER KISSED AN ANGEL		
	SLEEPY LAGOON		POINCIANA (SONG OF THE TREE)
LOUIS JORDAN	IS YOU IS, OR IS YOU AIN'T (MA' BABY)		SPEAK LOW
STAN KENTON	EV'RY TIME WE SAY GOODBYE		A STRING OF PEARLS
	THERE IS NO GREATER LOVE		SUNRISE SERENADE
ANDY KIRK	UNTIL THE REAL THING COMES ALONG	**THELONIOUS MONK**	EVERYTHING HAPPENS TO ME
GENE KRUPA	VIOLETS FOR YOUR FURS	**WES MONTGOMERY**	CARAVAN
KAY KYSER	ON A SLOW BOAT TO CHINA		DEARLY BELOVED
	WHO WOULDN'T LOVE YOU		GOD BLESS THE CHILD
GERTRUDE LAWRENCE	MY SHIP		I'M JUST A LUCKY SO AND SO
PEGGY LEE	EV'RYTHING I LOVE	**LEE MORGAN**	DAY BY DAY
	GOLDEN EARRINGS	**RAY NOBLE**	I HADN'T ANYONE TILL YOU
	WHY DON'T YOU DO RIGHT (GET ME SOME MONEY TOO!)		I'VE GOT YOU UNDER MY SKIN
		CHARLIE PARKER	ALL THE THINGS YOU ARE
	YOU'RE EASY TO DANCE WITH		EASY TO LOVE (A/K/A YOU'D BE SO EASY TO LOVE)
MICHEL LEGRAND	THE LAST TIME I SAW PARIS		I CAN'T GET STARTED WITH YOU
ABBEY LINCOLN	THE NEARNESS OF YOU		I DIDN'T KNOW WHAT TIME IT WAS
ELLA LOGAN	SOMETHING I DREAMED LAST NIGHT		I'LL WALK ALONE
GUY LOMBARDO	THE FOLKS WHO LIVE ON THE HILL		LOVER MAN (OH, WHERE CAN YOU BE?)
JIMMIE LUNCEFORD	BABY, WON'T YOU PLEASE COME HOME		MY HEART BELONGS TO DADDY
	FOR DANCERS ONLY		ON A SLOW BOAT TO CHINA
WYNTON MARSALIS	HOW ARE THINGS IN GLOCCA MORRA	**OSCAR PETERSON**	COME SUNDAY
MARY MARTIN	MY HEART BELONGS TO DADDY		GOOD-BYE
TONY MARTIN	IT'S A BLUE WORLD		I CONCENTRATE ON YOU
MAUREEN McGOVERN	RIGHT AS THE RAIN		IN THE STILL OF THE NIGHT
JOHNNY MERCER	CANDY		SATURDAY NIGHT IS THE LONELIEST NIGHT OF THE WEEK
	ONE FOR MY BABY (AND ONE MORE FOR THE ROAD)		SOMEDAY MY PRINCE WILL COME
			SWINGING ON A STAR
		TEDDY POWELL	LET'S GET LOST

DJANGO REINHARDT	NUAGES		THERE'S A SMALL HOTEL
LEO REISMAN	BEWITCHED	**JO STAFFORD**	I LOVE YOU
SONNY ROLLINS	THE HOUSE I LIVE IN		IT COULD HAPPEN TO YOU
	THERE WILL NEVER BE ANOTHER YOU		LONG AGO (AND FAR AWAY)
	THIS LOVE OF MINE	**SONNY STITT**	CHEROKEE (INDIAN LOVE SONG)
	WILL YOU STILL BE MINE		LONG AGO (AND FAR AWAY)
JIMMY ROWLES	THE LADY'S IN LOVE WITH YOU	**ART TATUM**	COME RAIN OR COME SHINE
ARTIE SHAW	I DON'T WANT TO WALK WITHOUT YOU		JITTERBUG WALTZ
GEORGE SHEARING	A LOVELY WAY TO SPEND AN EVENING	**JACK TEAGARDEN**	I GOTTA RIGHT TO SING THE BLUES
	MOONLIGHT BECOMES YOU	**MEL TORME**	AREN'T YOU GLAD YOU'RE YOU
	A SINNER KISSED AN ANGEL		A LOVELY WAY TO SPEND AN EVENING
DINAH SHORE	DEARLY BELOVED		NOBODY'S HEART
	I'LL WALK ALONE	**McCOY TYNER**	SPEAK LOW
	YOU'D BE SO NICE TO COME HOME TO		SWEET AND LOVELY
ZOOT SIMS	MY SILENT LOVE	**SARAH VAUGHAN**	I DON'T KNOW WHY (I JUST DO)
	PENNIES FROM HEAVEN		IMAGINATION
FRANK SINATRA	ALL OR NOTHING AT ALL		THINKING OF YOU
	ALL THROUGH THE DAY		WHY CAN'T I?
	BE CAREFUL, IT'S MY HEART		YOU'RE BLASÉ
	DAY BY DAY	**FATS WALLER**	JITTERBUG WALTZ
	FULL MOON AND EMPTY ARMS	**DINAH WASHINGTON**	WHAT A DIFF'RENCE A DAY MADE
	THE HOUSE I LIVE IN	**ETHEL WATERS**	STORMY WEATHER (KEEPS RAININ' ALL THE TIME)
	I COULDN'T SLEEP A WINK LAST NIGHT		
	I SHOULD CARE	**MARGARET WHITING**	COME RAIN OR COME SHINE
	I'LL BE SEEING YOU	**LEE WILEY**	MY FUNNY VALENTINE
	IF I LOVED YOU	**TEDDY WILSON**	THAT OLD FEELING
	IT NEVER ENTERED MY MIND		THIS YEAR'S KISSES
	ONE FOR MY BABY (AND ONE MORE FOR THE ROAD)	**PHIL WOODS**	WAIT TILL YOU SEE HER
	PEOPLE WILL SAY WE'RE IN LOVE		
	SATURDAY NIGHT IS THE LONELIEST NIGHT OF THE WEEK		
	STORMY WEATHER (KEEPS RAININ' ALL THE TIME)		
CAROL SLOANE	I'LL TAKE ROMANCE		
	SOMETHING TO LIVE FOR		
	YOU'RE NEARER		
JOHNNY SMITH	SENTIMENTAL JOURNEY		